Cherokee Plants

and their uses —

a 400 year history

Paul B. Hamel & Mary U. Chiltoskey

ACKNOWLEDGEMENTS

We wish to express our gratitude to the many people who have helped in the development of this book. Mr. Stephen Richmond of the Indian Arts and Crafts Board introduced the authors and secured photographs for their use. We want to thank F. L. Hiser Jr., Diane Hamel and David Moyer for their support. Libbi Lambert provided most of the drawings. G. B. Chiltoskey, Rebecca Grant, Ollie Jumper, and Dr. Aaron Sharp gave their able help and assistance in translating and deciphering the Indian names of plants. Craig DeWitt and Becky Kellington did an enormous amount of sorting and identifying plants and sources. Mary Kay Hamel and Dr. Harriet Holman were patient and helpful editors. Beverly Korst served as editor, proof reader, and layout artist. Dr. J. Page Crouch of the Graphic Art Laboratory of Clemson University's Department of Industrial Education gave freely of his time. The picture on the title page is G. B. Chiltoskey's work; the cover is Beverly Korst's work.

The authors accept responsibility for errors.

We dedicate this book to the Cherokee people who made it possible by their reverence for their environment and their ability to live as one with nature. Especially Hester Reagan who first showed Mary Chiltoskey this path.

Hester Reagan

"And God said, 'Let the earth bring forth grass, the herb yielding seed, and the fruit yielding fruit after its kind, whose seed is in itself, upon the earth': and it was so.

And the earth brought forth grass, and herb yielding seed after his kind, and the tree yielding fruit, whose seed was in itself, after his kind: and God saw that it was good.

And God said, 'Behold, I have given you every herb bearing seed, which is upon the face of all the earth, and every tree, in which is the fruit of a tree yielding seed; to you it shall be for meat.' "

Genesis 1:11-12, 29

INTRODUCTION

This book is an attempt to help complete the story of the Cherokee people, their relationship with each other and with their environment. To accomplish this we are dealing with the plants and some of the uses made of them by the Cherokee people during the past 400 years. Some of the uses have gradually passed; many of the rituals related to medicine plants and their healing have already been lost for lack of the right people to carry them forward. Indeed, some of the knowledge of one of the authors, Mary Chiltoskey, could not be shared even with the other author. She explains:

"As I ponder, and even bemoan, the passing of the knowledge once a part of the older Cherokees' use and ritual connected with the plants about them, I am reminded of something my brother-in-law told me about some of the things practiced by his parents. This knowledge that he tried to pass on to me will have to end with me. Why? Not because I am too selfish to share it, not because I disbelieve it, but because when I try to tell someone else, it is only a collection of words put together in sentences. The meaning of each word can be understood by another but the idea cannot be communicated by me to anyone else. I know what my brother-in-law meant, but when I use the same words in the same sentences they lack some inner meaning that he gave them. So I say that this bit of knowledge must go when I go."

Much of the material in this book came through conversations of older people at Cherokee, North Carolina, with Mary Chiltoskey during her more than thirty years of working and living on the Qualla Boundary (commonly called "Cherokee Indian Reservation"). A few direct quotations from "hard to get" books are used. Many of the plants still grow bravely amidst so-called civilization, to be recognized by an occasional keenly observant Cherokee who will delight in recounting the uses made of such plants by a foreparent.

This book is organized into two sections. The first section contains general information on how and why plants are used. Our concept of the spirit of the Cherokees' relationship to their environment is presented here. Please accept and observe this spirit when you use this book.

The second section contains lists of plants from the earliest recorded contacts of Cherokees with other peoples. This can be used in conjunction with a good wildflower or tree guide to appreciate southern Appalachian forests as seen through the eyes of a Cherokee.

Please observe the same principles of conservation as they did with things in their environment. Never take the first, or second, or third plant you find, nor take what cannot be used, nor take more than can be used. Had the Cherokees not observed these precepts, their land would hold no more mysteries. Can we afford to do less for those who will follow?

PAUL B. HAMEL

EXERCISE EXTREME CAUTION

Any attempts to use the plants in the lists that follow must be done with extreme caution. If you must experiment with these or other native remedies, you do so at your own risk. The Cherokee people called on their medicine man. He was their expert in the use of plant remedies.

Their efforts made this book possible . . .

Paul B. Hamel

Mary U. Chiltoskey

Rebecca Grant

G. B. Chiltoskey

Ollie Jumper

TABLE OF CONTENTS

PLANTS IN RELIGION AND MEDICINE

When we have some knowledge of the Cherokees' religion, of the scope of the medicine man's role, and an awareness of their medicine then we can more readily accept the fact that their beliefs were valid for them. These were the principles that guided their actions and they lived their day to day lives in close accord with them.

RELIGION

The Cherokee religion has not been the subject of any published studies through the years so we can say very little on the subject except that they believed in one Great Spirit.

The medicine man, or shaman, was a religious leader and an intermediary between the realms of the physical and the spiritual. Medicine men were able to make these contacts because of their special ability to communicate with their God. It is possible that Indians, or perhaps only their medicine men had the ability to communicate with the special forces in their environment. It is more likely that all people have these abilities but have neglected, or chosen not, to use them.

MEDICINE MEN

Medicine men possibly had a natural ability, but they refined their vocation by means of an apprenticeship. Much of their information was secretive and closely guarded, generally told only to selected apprentices. Most likely information on the use of plants was traded or shared with their peers. Apprentices learned by listening, observing and helping.

Anthropologists have determined that an individual medicine man may know three hundred to four hundred plants and their specific uses. Recently Amoneeta Sequoyah, a well known Cherokee medicine man, told L. C. Tankerskey Jr., a reporter for the Pickens, South Carolina Sentinel, he knew six hundred forty two medicinal plants. The accumulated knowledge of several medicine men in a village might reach eight hundred or more plants.

MEDICINE

The role of plants in Cherokee medicine is illustrated by the story of the Origin of Disease and Medicine. This story was first recorded by James Mooney of the United States Bureau of American Ethnology in 1890 in THE SACRED FORMUALS OF THE CHEROKEES.

Origin Of Disease And Medicine

"In the old days the beasts, birds, fishes, insects, and plants could all talk and they and the people lived together in peace and friendship. But as time went on the people increased so rapidly that . . . the poor animals found themselves beginning to be cramped for room . . . Man . . . begin to slaughter the larger animals . . . for their flesh or skins, while the smaller creatures, . . . were crushed . . . . So the animals resolved to consult upon measures for their common safety.

The Bears were the first to meet in council . . . and the old White Bear chief presided. After each in turn had complained of the way in which Man killed their friends . . . it was decided to begin war at once against him . . . . But when everything was ready and the first Bear stepped up to make the trial it was found that . . . his long claws . . . spoiled the shot . . . someone suggested that they might trim his claws . . . the old White Bear, objected, saying it was necessary that they should have long claws . . .

No one could think of any better plan so the old chief dismissed the council and the Bears dispersed . . . without having concerted any way to prevent the increase of the human race . . .

The Deer next held council under their chief, the Little Deer, and after some talk decided to send rheumatism to every hunter who should kill one of them unless he took care to ask their pardon for the offense . . .

Next came the Fishes and Reptiles, who had their own complaints against Man. They held their council together and determined to make victims dream . . .

Finally the Birds, Insects, and smaller animals came together . . . the Grubworm was chief of the council. It was decided that each in turn should give an opinion, and then they would vote on the question as to whether or not man was guilty. Seven votes should be enough to condemn him . . .

They began to devise and name so many new diseases one after another, that had not their invention failed them, no one of the human race would have been able to survive . . .

When the Plants, who were friendly to man heard what had been done by the animals, they determined to defeat the latter's evil designs. Each Tree, Shrub, and Herb, down even to the Grasses and Mosses, agreed to furnish a cure for some one of the diseases named, and each said: 'I shall appear to help Man when he calls upon me in his need.' Thus came medicine . . ."

A Cherokee's concept of Nun-wa-ti, medicine, is likely to include contacting a greater power for aid. Cherokee medicine involved home remedies and asking the medicine man for advise and treatment. Cherokee medicine had an additional aspect: the inter-relationship of religion and medicine.

Some remedies were probably widely known and used by the people. Various plants called "snakeroot" were known to be a cure for snakebite. Some of the lichens became known as blood leather from their use in stopping the flow of blood from wounds. If a person worked too hard he might make a poultice of the seven-bark hydrangea to ease the aches and pains.

When the home treatment did not effect a cure a medicine man was called. He was available to help in cases that were more serious, or prolonged than usual. He had the special talents and knowledge for finding, preparing, and administering the proper remedy. A clever medicine man knew when a complaint wasn't a physical illness but rather a lack of attention from others. He inspired confidence and applied the salve of attention to the wounded ego.

James Mooney was skeptical of the medicinal properties of the plants used. He compared a list of twenty Cherokee medicinal plants with those listed in the pharamaceutical directory of the day, United States Dispensatory. He found twenty-five percent of the Cherokee plants were used as the Dispensatory recommended. Another sixty percent were either not listed or were used incorrectly according the the Dispensatory. The rest of the medicinal plants were used in ways that were difficult to judge correct or incorrect from the Dispensatory.

When faced with a very difficult case the medicine man involved his patient in specific rituals and prayers. Some of these prayers, the Sacred Formulas of the Cherokees, have come to us mainly from A-Yun-i-ni, the Swimmer. Swimmer gave a list of some ninety formulas, written in the characters of the Sequoyah syllabary, to James Mooney.

The following formula for rheumatism is reproduced in tact from Mooneys, MYTHS OF THE CHEROKEE AND SACRED FORMULAS OF THE CHEROKEES.

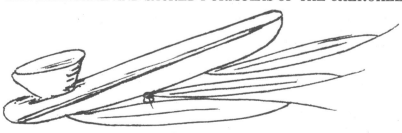

Photo by U.S. Dept. of the Interior, Indian Arts and Crafts Board

Double weave basket with lightening design. Made of river cane by Rowena Bradley an eastern Cherokee from the Qualla Boundary.

Asga'ya yûkanû'ⁿwĬ
Agĕ''ya Giagage'ĭ atătĬ';
agĕ''ya-nû yûkanû'ⁿwĬ
Asga'ya Gĭgage'ĭ atătĬ'.

Yû! Higĕ''ya Gĭgage'Ĭ tsûdante'lûhĬ gese'Ĭ. Ulsge'ta hi'tsanu'y'tani'leĬ'. Ha-Nûⁿdâgû'ⁿyĬ nûⁿta'tsûdălenû'hĬ gese'Ĭ. Gasgilâ' gigage'Ĭ tsusdi'ga tetsadĬ'ilĕ' detsala'siditĕ-gĕ'Ĭ. Hanâ'gwa usĬnuli'yu det-saldisi'yûĬ.

UtsĬ(nă')wa nu'tatanû'ⁿta. Usû'hita nutanû'na. UtsĬnă'wa-gwû nigûⁿtisge'stĬ.

(Degâ'sisisgû'ⁿĬ)—Hiă-gwû' nigaû' kanâhe'ta. Nû''kiha nagû'n-kw'tisgă' dagû'ⁿstiskû'Ĭ. Sâ'gwa nûⁿskwû'ta gûnstû'ⁿĬ agûnstagi's-kâĬ hûⁿtsatasgâ'Ĭ nû''kine-'nû ûⁿskwû'ta nû''kĬ nûⁿtsâtasgâ'Ĭ. Hiă-'nû' nû'ⁿwâtĬ: Egû'ⁿlĬ, Yâ'na-'nû Utsĕsdâ'gĬ, (U)wa'sgilĬ tsĬgĬ' Egû'ⁿlĬ, tă'lĬ tsinu'dalĕ'ha, Kâ'ga-'nû Asgû'ⁿtagĕ tsiûⁿnâ'sehâ'Ĭ, Da'yĬ-'nû Uwâ'yĬ tsiûⁿnâ'sehâ'Ĭ. Su'talĬ iyutale'gĬ unaste'tsa agâ'tĬ, uga'nawû-'nû' dagûnsta''tisgâ'Ĭ nû'ⁿwâtĬ asûⁿga'la'Ĭ. Usû'hĬ adanû'ⁿwâtĬ. nu''kĬ tsusû'hita dulsi'nisû'ⁿ adanû'ⁿwâtĬ. Ă'nawa'gi-'nû dilasula'gĬ gesû'ⁿĬ ûlĕ' tsĬkani'kaga'Ĭ gûw'sdi'-gwû utsawa'ta ă'nawa'-gwû-nû'.

Hiă-nû' gaktû'ⁿta gûlkwâ'gĬ tsusû'hita. Gû'ⁿwădana'datlahistĬ' nige'sûⁿna—Salâ'lĬ, gi''li-'nû, wĕ'sa-'nû, ă'tatsû-nû'; a'mă-'nû', anigĕ''ya-nû. Uda'lĬ' ya'kanûⁿwi'ya nû''kiha tsusû'hita unădană'lâtsi-tastĬ nige'sûⁿna. Gasgilâ'gi-'nû uwă'suⁿ-gwû' u'skĬladi'stĬ uwă'sû nû''kĬ tsusû'hită'. Disâ'i-'nû dega'sgilâ û'ⁿtsa nû'nă' uwa''tĬ yigesûĬ nû''kĬ tsusû'hita.

Translation.

AND THIS ALSO IS FOR TREATING THE CRIPPLER.

Yû! O Red Woman, you have caused it. You have put the intruder under him. Ha! now you have come from the Sun Land. You have brought the small red seats, with your feet resting upon them. Ha! now they have swiftly moved away from you. Relief is accomplished. Let it not be for one night alone. Let the relief come at once.

(Prescription)—*(corner note at top.)* If treating a man one must say *Red Woman*, and if treating a woman one must say *Red Man.*

This is just all of the prayer. Repeat it four times while laying on the hands. After saying it over once, with the hands on (the body of the patient), take off the hands and blow once, and at the fourth repetition blow four times. And this is the medicine. Egû'ⁿlĬ (a species of fern). Yâ'-na-Utsĕ'sta ("bear's bed," the Aspidium acrostichoideṣ or Christmas fern). *two* varieties of the soft-(leaved) Egû'ⁿlĬ (one, the small variety, is the Cinnamon fern, Osmunda cinnamonea), and what is called Kâ'ga Asgû'ⁿtagĕ ("crow's shin," the Adiantum pedatum or Maidenhair fern) and what is called Da'yĬ-Uwâ'yĬ ("beaver's paw"—not identified). Boil the roots of the six varieties together and apply the hands warm with the medicine upon them. Doctor in the evening. Doctor four consecutive nights. (The pay) is cloth and moccasins; or, if one does not have them, just a little dressed deerskin and some cloth.

And this is the tabu for seven nights. One must not touch a squirrel, a dog, a cat, the mountain trout, or women. If one is treating a married man they (*sic*) must not touch his wife for four nights. And he must sit on a seat by himself for four nights, and must not sit on the other seats for four nights.

Cherokee Alphabet.

D a	R e	T i	♂ o	O u	i v
S ga O ka	F ge	Y gi	A go	J gu	E gv
♂ ha	P he	♉ hi	F ho	Γ hu	Ꮻ hv
W la	C le	P li	G lo	M lu	ᏻ lv
♂ ma	Q me	H mi	♃ mo	Y mu	
Θ na Ꮱ hna G nah	Λ ne	h ni	Z no	Ꮓ nu	O hv
T qua	⟲ que	℘ qui	V quo	⟲ quu	ℰ quv
U sa ♂ s	♃ se	b si	♱ so	ℰ su	R sv
L da W ta	S de Ꮮ te	♃ di ♃ ti	V do	S du	♌ dv
♃ dla ♃ tla	L tle	C tli	♃ tlo	♃ tlu	P tlv
G tsa	V tse	Ir tsi	K tso	J tsu	C tsv
G wa	⟲ we	Θ wi	C wo	♃ wu	6 wv
⟲ ya	β ye	♃ yi	♃ yo	G yu	B yv

Sounds represented by Vowels.

a, as a in father, or short as a in rival   o, as aw in law, or short as o in not.
e, as a in hate, or short as e in met   u, as oo in fool, or short as u in pull.
i, as i in pique, or short as i in pit   v, as u in but, nasalized.

Consonant Sounds

g nearly as in English, but approaching to k. d nearly as in English but approaching to t. h k l m n q s t w y as in English. Syllables beginning with g except Ꮝ have sometimes the power of k. A S O are sometimes sounded to, tu, tv, and Syllables written with tl except Ꮯ sometimes vary to dl.

THE CHEROKEE ALPHABET

It is not known how or to what extent Cherokee medicine was effective in the present-day sense. It may not have worked at all unless the people were committed to their religion, and to their spiritual as well as practical relationship with their environment. And yet . . . . Cherokee medical methods worked for the Cherokee people. Perhaps the problems we have in understanding them and their usefulness may well be due to our being confronted with too much about the intellectual aspects.

PLANTS IN SOCIAL ACTIVITIES

A people's culture is a complex fabric woven from threads of its recreation, education, festivals, arbitration and most important its social organizations. The fabric of the Cherokee culture suffered two severe strains in the last century which nearly destroyed it. First, the native religion was supplemented by the Christian gospel, which disrupted the traditional ceremonial cycle. Secondly, the trauma of the Removal in the 1830's seriously damaged the traditional clan governing system and further disrupted the annual ceremonial ritual. Much of what is said about the festivals and of plants used in them cannot be verified by first-hand knowledge. Other information regarding ball-play and recreation has survived.

SOCIAL STRUCTURES

Cherokee society was organized into seven clans. A clan was an expanded family with right of inheritance and clan membership being determined through the maternal side of the family. Here are the names of the clans reproduced from four different sources: James Mooney in MYTHS OF THE CHEROKEE, William Gilbert in EASTERN CHEROKEE SOCIAL ORGANIZATION, J. Ed Sharpe in THE CHEROKEES PAST AND PRESENT, and Watty Chiltoskie in Mary Ulmer Chiltoskey's CHEROKEE WORDS.

Names of Cherokee Clans

Mooney	Gilbert	Chiltoskie	Sharpe	Translation
Ani'-Wa''ya	A-ni-wa-hi-ya	A-ni-wa-ya	A-ni-wa-yah	Wolf
Ani'-Kawi'	A-ni-ka-wi	A-ni-a-wi	A-ni-ka-wi	Deer
Ani'-Tsi'skwa	A-ni-dji-s-kwa	A-ni-tsi-s-qua	A-ni-tsi-s-kwa	Bird
Ani'-Wa'di	A-ni-wo-di	A-ni-wo-di	A-ni-wo-di	Red Paint
Ani'-Saha'ni	A-ni-sa-ho-ni	A-ni-sa-ho-ni	A-ni-sa-ho-ni	Blue Plant, Blue Holly
Ani'-Ga'tage'wi	A-ni-go-ti-ge-wi	A-ni-go-da-ge-wi	A-ni-ga-to-ge-wi	Wild Potato
Ani'-Gila'hi	A-ni-gi-lo-hi (Twister)	A-ni-gi-lo-gi (Panther)	A-ni-gi-lo-hi (Long hair)	No good translation

Clan membership gave structure and stability to peoples' lives by providing rules for social relationships such as who could marry whom and where to look for help. After the immediate family group of children, parents, and grandparents, the clan was the most important group to which a person belonged. The seven clan system of Cherokee society dictated that the council house in each town have seven sides with provisions to seat each clan separately. Wall-hangings woven of cane kept drafts off those people attending the meetings. Traditional designs woven into the mats probably indicated where each clan should sit. In addition to mats the council house in Oconaluftee Village in Cherokee, North Carolina, is furnished with dance masks, wands, and gourd dippers.

In the center of the council house the sacred fire burned continuously, fueled by seven different kinds of wood. We have two lists of council fire woods. One is from Tom Jumper, recalling woods used probably about 1900, and the other is from Watty Chiltoskie in the book CHEROKEE WORDS. The Jumper list includes beech, birch, hickory, locust, maple, oak, and sourwood, The Chiltoskie list has ash, beech, birch, hickory, locust, maple and oak. The woods used in the fire varied with the availability of different trees from place to place.

The strong native American tobacco was one of the most important plants used at council meetings. Pipes and the smoking of tobacco were reserved for special, ceremonial occasions among the Cherokee as among most other North American peoples. Pipes were smoked to signify agreement and accord of the people on the issues in question: both within the tribe and with other peoples. Pipe smoking honored all involved. Stems for ceremonial pipes were frequently made of sourwood because of the easily removable pith. The bowls of the pipes were fashioned of soapstone or clay.

Towns were organized under two different kinds of leadership, the White and the Red. The White was the leadership of peacetime, with a headman, a beloved woman, and a council of elders. The members of the council came from each of the clans; they were wise older men. The Red organization took over during times of emergency or war; they also had a headman, a war woman, and a council of men from the seven clans.

ARBITRATION

The ball-play, A-ne-tsa (little brother to war), was important to Cherokee people because it involved religious ritual and had political overtones. Coosawattee in north Georgia commemorates the peaceful settlement of a land dispute between the Cherokee and Creek nations by ball-play. The Cherokees won. To this day, the place is called Coosawattee, meaning the "old country of the Creeks."

Each team has two managers, called drivers because of the long hickory switches they carry, who are responsible for making sure the few rules are not violated. The object of the game is to throw or carry the ball through a goal marked by two green saplings. The goals lie about one hundred twenty yards apart on flat open ground. The game is played until one team scores twelve points. There is no time limit.

Every player carries two hickory ballsticks, shaped like long handled miniature tennis rackets strung with leather, Indian hemp or inner hickory bark. The sticks are approximately eighteen inches long. Players are required to use these to pick the ball up from the ground. The ball was about the size of a golfball, made of leather stuffed with deer hair; today it is made of rubber.

James Mooney's book, MYTHS OF THE CHEROKEE AND SACRED FORMULAS OF THE CHEROKEES, contains information about the rigorous training program of those early players. Today the rules are less strict. Workouts were conducted by a medicine man who used various plant materials in conjunction with the prescribed rituals. The men rubbed their limbs with preparations from such plants as the slippery elm to make themselves strong and slippery. The players, with the aid and direction of the medicine man prepared themselves spiritually, mentally, and physically.

Betting on the game was a serious affair and often bitterly contested. For this reason betting on the game and finally the game itself was outlawed for several decades in this century by white authorities.

FESTIVALS

As nearly as can be determined, six main festivals comprised the annual cycle. Those presented here were given by J. Ed. Sharpe in his book, THE CHEROKEES

PAST AND PRESENT. The cycle started in March, when the first new moon of spring was celebrated. The earliest roasting ears of sweet corn in August were met with So-lu-tsun-i-gi-s-ti-s-ti, the Green Corn ceremony. This was a festival not only of the Cherokee people but of all the southern tribes.

September brought two festivals, Do-na-go-hu-ni, the feast of ripe corn, and E-la-wa-ta-le-gi the Bush Feast. Nu-wa-ti-e-gwa, ceremony of the Great Moon occurred in October, followed by A-to-hu-na (the Celebration of Friendship) later in that month, or in November. Each of these festivals were accompanied by specific rituals, which included dances and involved the use of plants.

The festival of purification is likely to have occurred during one of the fall festivals. We cannot confirm the exact annual festival. On this occasion the people put out all the fires. Through the rites of the festival, a new sacred fire was consecrated and the fires in the homes were started from it. In addition to cleaning out the fireplaces and rekindling fires, it was the time for ritual cleansing of the people as well. This was accomplished in the Black Drink ceremony. Black drink is a tea or decoction of the dried baked leaves of either of two hollies, the yaupon or cassine. Originally, neither of these plants grew in Cherokee country; periodic trips to the coastal swamps of the Carolinas were necessary to gather them. Under favorable conditions each of the plants was later cultivated near Cherokee towns. Weak teas of these plants make a drink similar to coffee but stronger decoctions caused the drinker to vomit, hence to be cleansed and purified. Yaupon (ILEX VOMITORIA) is usually regarded as the more important of the two although both species were used. The people practiced their botany by function rather than by modern-day taxonomy.

EDUCATION

Dances are likely to have re-enacted historical events and generally instructed people about their environment and the things in it. Special dances required such equipment as masks, costumes, and musical instruments; gourd or turtleshell rattles and drums of hemlock or buckeye covered with ground hog skin were used. Many dances were totally lost during the last century.

Dances remembered by folks and still in use in the 1970s are: Ball, Bear, Beaver, Buffalo, Booger, Eagle, Friendship, Green Corn, Partridge (Quail). The dances show us that Cherokee women often danced while their men danced, though seldom with them. During the time when traditional Cherokee society was intact, education surpassed recreation as a primary reason for dancing. Masks were usually made of buckeye wood or other materials that could be shaped quite easily. Wands used in the eagle dance were made of cane or sourwood.

Though children lacked the structured schooling of the twentieth century, their learning opportunities were constant. They began by imitating adults and as their skills progressed they were given new goals. Story time was one form of instruction. The following is one of Mary Chiltoskey's favorite stories about one of the plants found in this region.

"Before selfishness came into the world — that was a long time ago — the Cherokee people were happy sharing the hunting and fishing places with their neighbors. All this changed when Selfishness came into the world and men began to quarrel. The Cherokees quarreled with tribes on the east. Finally the chiefs of several tribes met in council to try to settle the dispute. They smoked the pipe and continued to quarrel for seven days and seven nights. This displeased the Great Spirit because people are not supposed to smoke the pipe until they make peace. As he looked upon the old men with heads bowed, he decided to do something to remind people to smoke the pipe only at the time they make peace.

The Great Spirit turned the old men into grayish flowers we now call 'Indian Pipes' and made them grow where friends and relatives have quarreled. He made the smoke hang over these mountains until all people all over the world learn to live together in peace.

This story's lesson is still current and valid today.

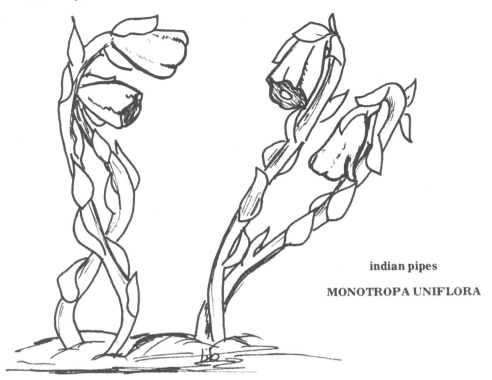

indian pipes

MONOTROPA UNIFLORA

RECREATION

Among the games the Cherokees played, marbles and Chung-ke were outdoor games; while the popular butterbean game could be played indoors. These and other games the people played were less an occasion for competition than for socializing.

Hardly any Cherokee was without marbles in his pocket. Made of pottery clay and hardened in the fire, they gave a person the chance to play and bet with his friends during leisure time. Small marbles could be fired while moist; if larger they had to be thoroughly dry before firing. These were usually made several at a time, in case one or more broke during the firing. Changing the kind of clay, and the woods used in the fire altered the color of the marbles.

The Chung-ke game was played by men or boys using stout sticks and a special disc, the Chung-ke stone. The stone was about five inches in diameter, and concave on both sides. One player rolled the stone on its edge down an incline onto a flat area. The others threw their sticks at it as it rolled; knocking the stone over was an automatic win. Otherwise the player whose stick was closest to the stone when it stopped rolling was the winner.

The butterbean game was another pastime. Two teams of any number could play and the equipment was simple. The game was played with six half-butterbeans, twenty four corn kernels as counters, and a flat basket about eighteen inches square and approximately two and a half inches deep. The baskets were likely to have been made of the inner hickory bark, cane, or oak splits.

To play the butterbean game, a person put the six half-butterbeans in the basket, flipped them into the air, and caught them. Each flip that scored gave the scorer another turn. Only three combinations were counted: 1. all flat, light sides — six points; 2. all round, dark sides — four points; 3. a single side of one color and five of the other color — two points. The game began with all the counters in a neutral pot and ended when one of the teams had all the counters. The game brought people together for enjoyment.

Originally in midwinter and more recently at Christmas time, this game came into its own. On Christmas eve it was traditional for the men to play against the women. The losers gathered wood for the women to cook Christmas dinner. Winners were entitled to use soot to smut the losers' faces.

Cherokee children played with toys that imitated their adult roles. The girls had cornshuck or rag dolls and toy Ka-no-na's; the boys had small bows, blowguns, and ballsticks. Their play taught them their adult roles.

PLANTS IN DAY TO DAY LIVING

The Cherokees as a group have enjoyed an intimate and benefical relationship with their environment for centuries. Nature and natural things filled the people's day to day life. Using a technology different from ours in the twentieth century, the people utilized the things that they had to make what they needed. Their foods, shelters and home furnishings, household utensils, light and heat, weapons, even their articles of personal adornment, were products of the forest. One Cherokee story illustrates how closely the people felt themselves to be part of,members of, their forest ecosystem. Told to Mary Chiltoskey by several Cherokee persons this version is presented essentially as she did to a group of young people who asked "Why do we have corn?"

"This story is about the first man. You know the Great One made four men before he made the Cherokee, and put him here in the mountains?

He gave the man all the world he could reach. The Great One told the man about the animals and how he might use them when he needed them. He would use the deer for food, clothing, implements, bowstrings, and thread to sew his clothes. Part of the animal would be medicine and one of the bones would be used to shape arrowheads. The deer tribe understood that they were to share some of their members with him.

The Great One didn't say anything about sport hunting, or hunting just for fun; but he did give man bow and arrows, and showed how to use them. He also put a brain in man's head but the man just sort of wandered around, went here and yonder, not doing much of anything. At first he got only the deer that he needed to live; but after awhile he started taking pot shots at the deer and the other animals. Maybe he was lonely. Finally, so many of the animals were being killed uselessly that they thought they'd better do something about it.

So one day the deer, the A-wi, called on the Great One up in Ga-lun-la-ti. They said, 'Look here, we thought man was decent, that the world would be better because of him. You gave him a brain and we thought he'd use it. We hoped he would do something worthwhile, build a home, work, learn how to do things. Well he hasn't. Just look at him lying over there on the ground asleep in the sunshine with his face turned to the sky. The dumbest animal has more sense than that. When an animal wants to go to sleep he finds himself a sheltered place, under a tree root, in a cave, in some brush, even on the underside of a leaf. For all his brain, that man doesn't have the sense of the dumbest animal.'

The Great One was surprised. He looked at the man and thought, 'Well, they have a point, that is a pretty sorry looking fellow. I'll have to do something to help him. I wonder what?' He pondered for awhile.

'Oh, I know what's the matter with him,' he said, 'he's lonesome. I have to send

14

him a companion. You, deer, and other animals, just stand back. I'll take care of this right away.'

So from the heart of the man lying there, the Great One made a plant grow straight up toward the sky. Graceful green blades grew up on the sides of the plant and bent over so prettily. Where the blades grew from the stalks, ears with grain developed with lovely shucks on them. At the top there developed the most beautiful creature you could ever imagine.

The man thought he was dreaming. He looked up at her and said, 'Oh, isn't she pretty! I would love to have her for my companion. I wish I were awake and this were true. I would take her and love her. I'd work so hard, build a home for us. I could be somebody. I could be a worthwhile person.' As soon as he wished that, the Great Spirit made him realize that he wasn't dreaming at all. That was the companion that the Great One had created for him. She was his. So he crawled out from under that stalk of corn . . . (Next time you're around growing corn look and see where he crawled out) . . . and helped this beautiful one down using the most delightful manners. You can't imagine the good manners he used, and no one had taught him. He claimed her for his own and together they went away to make themselves a home.

Corn Maiden

Before they left, the first woman wanted to take some of the corn with her to remind her of her heritage. So she pulled two ears from that stalk. It was Se-lu, the first corn. You might think that they made some cornbread that night but they didn't because she did not know that corn was something good to eat. She thought it was just something pretty so she planted some out in front of the house. You know, like we plant roses, daffodils, and other things today. Every year for several years it grew up and she enjoyed looking at it and was satisfied.

One morning she looked out into the yard and, would you believe it, there was a bird eating some of the nice juicy seeds of the corn. It was a big bird, Gun-na, the wild turkey, sacred bird for things on earth. She knew that if Gun-na ate it, people could too. Now it was the time of the year that the corn was green, in the milk stage, so that night for supper she picked and cooked the first roasting ears ever served.

15

Since they now had corn to add to their deer meat, wild greens, and fish, they ate well and things went along just fine for awhile. They were healthy and happy. Then one morning the woman became angry. The man didn't know why she was angry and just went on with his work. She went stomping out of the door with her head held high and her feet hitting the ground good and hard. He thought, 'She'll get outside in the air and sunshine for a few minutes and then come back and everything will be fine.'

Several minutes went by. She didn't come back. So he went to the door to look and there she was going over the first mountain over yonder. 'Oh, my goodness, look how far away she is already. She's very angry,' dropping his tools on the floor, he started running after her. His heart was heavy.

You know what it's like when you get angry. You can turn that anger into energy, and if you don't spout off your mouth then you have a lot of energy to do what you are doing. When your heart is heavy, like his was, then your feet are heavy, too. By the time he got to the top of the first mountain there she was going over the second one. He went down the mountain, crossed the branch and struggled up the second one. She was already on top of the next one.

'Oh, no, I can't take it. She's leaving me,' he said, collapsing on a rock. Then he did something that people have always done when they have a problem that's too big for them to handle. 'Oh, Great One,' he cried, 'come help me.'

'Whats your problem?' The Great One was right there.

'Oh, she's leaving me. The companion you gave me is leaving me.'

'What'd you do?'

'I didn't do anything.'

'Maybe it's something you DIDN'T do.'

'Oh, I don't know. She's leaving me. I can't stand it. Please help me.'

'Okay, you just sit here on this rock and rest a little while, but not too long. Then come and follow me.'

The Great One raced ahead as only he can do until he was right behind her. 'Let's see, what can I do to make her stop?' He made the beautiful sarvis tree grow up right beside the path with the first white flowers of spring. She walked right past. He made the flowers mature into juicy red berries. We call them Juneberries because they ripen in June. Again she didn't stop.

So he made huckleberry bushes grow up along the path, just covered with ripe juicy berries, the kind you can eat all you want and not get sick. Right through them she went, scattering berries everywhere on the ground. 'She is angry. I'm going to have to get tricky with her.'

He made blackberry bushes with thorns grow beside the path and right on the path. She walked right over them. Didn't stop when they tore her dress and snagged and cut her leg. She didn't even bend over to stop the blood trickling down her leg.

'What can I do now? Let's see, what do you have to do to get over being angry? You have to bend your knee and bow your head. How can I get her to do that? Maybe I can get to her weakest part, her most vulnerable part, her curiosity? (Some say that's a woman's strongest point.)

The Great One then made a big patch of berries, little red heart shaped ones, grow all over the place, down close to the ground. The woman marched right through them, but before she'd gone very far, the sweet fragrance of the crushed berries caught her attention. She became very curious about the smell and looked down to see what it was. They smelled so good she just had to have a taste so she knelt down and tried one. They were good.

Just as quick as that her anger went away. Her first thought was, 'I'll pick some for my husband.' So she began picking them and the Great One made that berry patch grow back in the direction her husband was coming. She picked some poplar leaves and made a cup to hold the berries.

Pretty soon her husband came up the trail. She ran to meet him as soon as she saw him. She could scarcely wait to share what she'd found with him. She fed him a berry and then herself a berry until the double-handful she'd gathered was gone. She was a good housewife so the next thing she thought was, 'What shall we have for supper? I know, we'll take some of these berries home.'

Her husband saw the berries and knew that was how the Great One had caused her to stop for him. 'This little plant saved my life. It brought my wife back to me,' he thought, 'I'll pick two or three of the little vines to take home and plant in the yard with the corn.' Then they went back home gathering strawberries, for that's what they were.

When they arrived home that night he stopped out in the yard and planted the strawberry plants near the corn. She went inside, thinking, 'Oh, how could I have left my home, my security, and my husband, all because I was angry? I don't even remember why. I'm going to keep a few of these special berries around the house to remind me of what I almost threw away.' So she looked around for a place to put them. They looked like they might spoil pretty fast. She spied a pottery jar on the shelf half full of honey they'd gathered last year. Honey keeps for a long time so she dropped the biggest of the berries into the honey until the jar was full.

Some say that strawberry preserves were born that day. Maybe they were. What we can say for sure is that every well-meaning Cherokee housewife keeps strawberries in the house year-round, whether, frozen, or canned, or preserved, or fresh. Girls, make sure that you have plenty of strawberries in your house. They'll keep it happy, they'll keep it peaceful. Boys be sure that you give your wives a way to get those strawberries."

FOOD

Any day of the year wild plants are obtainable and can be made an important part of the diet. Starting in January or a little before wild greens are available. Cresses are earliest, followed by ramps. So-cha-ni, the green-headed coneflower, is likely to be next, followed in their season by lambsquarters, and numerous other plants that make good cooked salad. Pokeweed is one of the most difficult to prepare. The root and fibrous stems of the plant are poisonous. If the tender shoots are boiled in fresh water several times, then fried in grease with an egg, the taste is worth the effort.

Summer brought fruits and berries, and all were eaten. Some of the plants get their names from their uses. The name of the flowering raspberry, Yun-oo-gi-s-ti, means "what the bear eats." Among the fruits were those of the passionflower, often called old field apricot, and the fleshy lining of the seed pods of the honey locust tree.

In autumn the many trees of the forest produced a good crop of seeds and nuts. Chestnuts were by far the most favored, until an Oriental blight destroyed virtually all of the trees early in this century. Raw or roasted, in soup, or boiled in bread they were a prize. Roasted and ground they made a substitute for coffee. Other delicious nuts came from walnut, hickory, butternut, hazel, and chinquapin trees.

Whether you accept the Cherokee story of its origin or not, corn was undoubtedly the most important plant food. The Cherokee wife might boil or roast fresh corn. She would grind dried corn into meal for frying, or boil it with hardwood ashes to make hominy. Hominy might be eaten as it was, or ground into grits. In one form or another corn was part of nearly every meal. Corn, Se-lu, was ground using a long hickory or oak stick. The larger, heavy end was used for weight at the top rather than for grinding. The grains were held in an upright hollowed-out oak log called a Ka-no-na. A requirement of the wood for the Ka-no-na is that it not add any special flavor to the corn.

Beans and squash are also very prominent foods. The native American beans present a great many varieties. When European beans are added, the diversity of these foods is remarkable. The list includes October or cherry beans, pinto beans, Jack (Jackson Wonder Bush) beans, butterbeans, Lima beans, clay and other field peas, cornfield beans (Kentucky Wonder), pole beans, and others. A Cherokee girl learned to prepare green beans; a bean, corn and hickory nut soup called Ga-na-tsi;

17

to bake bean bread; to dry them into leather breeches; to make pickled beans; or to make a three-bean salad. The squashes include summer varieties and pumpkins. Butternut is a common squash, as is the candy roaster, a squash developed in Cherokee, North Carolina, early in this century. Squashes are eaten fried or baked; pumpkins can be diced into soups and casseroles.

Related to the squashes is the bottlegourd, LAGENARIA, used primarily for carrying utensils like dippers, and for storage jars. Frequently, writers have said no one ever eats gourds, but today there is a woman in Cherokee, North Carolina, who every year prepares a meal of the first tender young gourds.

Last among the native, cultivated foods was the white potato. Developed first in Peru, it had found its way to Cherokee country before 1600 AD.

Plants brought to the Cherokee lands by African or European settlers were added to the peoples' diet. Cabbage, sweet potato, apples, mustard greens, turnips, pear, peaches, melons, and many others got onto the menu this way. These, together with the others mentioned before, form the staples, the mainstays, of the Cherokee diet.

Water was the most common beverage. Frequently a little spice wood, sassafras, or sumach was added to make a hot tea. Fruit juices were used in season. Ah-me-ge-i, the partially fermented liquor made from coarsely beaten hominy corn boiled in water, was the strongest Cherokee drink. This was a welcome refreshment after working all day in the fields. Its alcohol content was negligible.

These were their usual foods, but a great number of other things to eat were obtainable near the home. Yellowjacket grubs and other insect larvae were among those. The Cherokee people knew a great deal about food and eating even though they may not have been familiar with the nice words of nutrition.

SHELTER AND HOME FURNISHINGS

When DeSoto came to Cherokee country in 1540 he found the people living in pole houses of straight saplings covered with plaited mats of cane and other sticks. The mats were plastered with a coat of mud and the roof was of thatch.

The people began living in log houses in the eighteenth century when iron tools became common. A favorite wood was tulip poplar because it was tall, straight, without limbs, and easy to work. Adult trees from mature forests worked better than second-growth trees which grew too fast. This was a new use for the poplar, Tsi-yu, whose name is also the word for canoe.

Trees for canoes were taken down by burning away the base with a small fire and then hollowed out ever so slowly using fire and a stone or iron scraper. The entire process might take as long as six months.

Frame and plank houses were common among the people in the late nineteenth century. Oak and chestnut were popular building materials, including shakes for roofing material. Today concrete block, brick or frame houses are found in the same percentages among the Cherokee people as found elsewhere.

A variety of woods have been used for household furniture. The earliest beds were piles of boughs which were replaced later by wooden frames when metal tools became available. Mattresses have been ticking filled with straw, either rye or wheat; or with cornshucks. A progression from simple to more complex construction has occurred for other furniture, such as tables, benches, and chairs. One stated preference calls for buckeye wood for baby cradles.

HOUSEHOLD UTENSILS

The Cherokee housewife has at various times used gourds, baskets, pottery, wooden utensils, and eventually metal ones. Gourd containers for carrying and storing were perhaps among the oldest, because they could be grown and used with minor modifications.

Baskets are probably next oldest. Some of the finest craftsmanship of the Cherokee

18

people is that devoted to the making of baskets, the traditional materials for basket work are cane, white oak when metal tools became available; more recently Japanese honeysuckle vines and maple. The cane and oak were used for heavy-duty and all-purpose wares, while the honeysuckle and maple are used primarily for light and ornamental pieces intended for the tourist trade.

River cane is a very important plant in Cherokee culture. It has long been used for blowguns, arrowshafts, candles, mats and baskets. Growing throughout Cherokee lands, cane reaches its greatest height of fifteen to thirty feet along river bottoms. Formerly such large, dense growths called canebrakes were very common. The Reedy River, which flows through downtown Greenville, South Carolina, received its name from the many acres of canebrakes growing along its banks when the town was first settled about 1780. Today they are much scarcer.

The woman intending to use cane for baskets would go to a nearby canebrake, collect a number of the stems six feet or more long and quarter them. She would peel off the inside until all her strips were flexible and of even thickness. They were then ready for dyeing and use.

The natural color of the cane ranges from a delicate green to a rich brown or nearly rust color. Many baskets were made using the natural color, but as the ease with which the cane accepts and hold dyes became known the people used dyed cane to weave intricate patterns. Four dyes have been used for centuries — the brown of walnut, the black of butternut, the rich orange of bloodroot, and a delicate yellow from yellowroot.

A large pot filled with water and alternate layers of cane and dye materials was boiled until the desired color was obtained. Urine and wood ashes lye were early mordants for setting the color; alum has replaced them more recently. The colors are deepest at the bottom of the pot. Successive batches of splits dyed with the same material are successively paler. Commercial dyes are sometimes used today to satisfy the tourists' desire for fire engine red and flat black.

The dyed cane was then woven into baskets or into mats used for wall-hangings which stopped drafts in the Cherokee home. Several weaves were used, and a variety of basket types produced. Some baskets were flat or deep as the need dictated, others were loosely woven for sieves, and a very special basket could even be made to hold water. This special basket was of the famous double weave. There was a basket for every need.

Designs on the baskets portrayed important clan and tribal symbols. Many of the designs were lost during the Removal, others are being forgotten and lost today as the culture changes and as these materials are no longer readily available.

Like cane, small white oak splits accept and hold dye very well. Oak is more sturdy, making excellent fishbaskets, heavyduty wares, and sieves. Whatever the desired product, choice of the tree is critical. The best white oaks for making baskets are found growing on north slopes. They have smooth flat bark that doesn't spiral, and are about twenty years old. Trees are cut, split into eighths, both the bark and the heartwood are removed. With skill the remainder can be split into strips as narrow as one fourth inch and as thin as ten or twelve thousandths of an inch. As long as they are kept damp the split, or splints, are pliable and easy to work. The preparation of maple is similar to that of oak, but since it is less durable and has a high sheen it is woven primarily into decorative pieces.

Honeysuckle is easier to gather and use than other materials. The vines have become common in sunny places, and the stems can be obtained any time "when the snakes are gone." The papery bark and tougher cambium must be removed after boiling. The vines are then dyed and worked as the other basket materials.

An old story tells that one day a Cherokee woman was cooking in a water tight basket and when she patched a hole in it with mud, pottery was born. The people began making coiled pottery with designs scratched or pressed into the clay. Good clays were available along stream banks where the very fine particles had accumulated at the ground water table. The clays are prepared by drying, grinding to powder, tempering with broken pots or other materials, and wetting again for use.

Firing the pots with different woods produces different colors of pottery. Hickories and oaks make the lightest colored pottery. Adding a little pine to the fire darkens the pieces. If a potter wanted a very black color, the fire was covered with leaves and other green materials.

LIGHT AND HEAT

Light for a Cherokee home came primarily from the sun. After sunset, the people used sections of cane, fat pine knots, or dried rolled up mullein leaves saturated with meat grease to illuminate their activities. Electricity does the job today. As new knowledge becomes available, the Cherokee people adopt what is compatible with their lifestyle.

For all purpose firewoods, softwoods like the pines smoke while oaks and hickories, the hard woods, produce hotter, cleaner fires. Chestnut and hemlock crack and pop as they burn, sending hot sparks flying about. Oaks and hickories are not guilty of this.

WEAPONS AND TOOLS

Before the advent of firearms, a Cherokee hunter relied on two silent weapons, his bow and arrows for big game, and blowgun for small game. The bow was usually about six feet long, made of very durable yellow locust wood. Cherokees named the locust tree from the color of its wood; modern-day botanist call it black locust. The bow was strung with deer or bear gut. The arrows were made of cane or sourwood, feathered with turkey feathers, and tipped with stone points.

The blowgun, used for small game like robins, jays and sometimes for squirrels, was a hollowed-out cane six or more feet long. A long stem about an inch in diameter was cut, hung with a weight on it, and allowed to dry thoroughly. Though mostly hollow, the joints of the cane are solid and must be removed. Originally the joints were burned out by means of a slow process. A long straight stick, like dogwood, with live coals on the end was pushed into the cane; or small live coals were dropped into the cane and pressed down with a stick. Later on, iron rods were heated in the fire and used to burn out the joints. After the cane had been hollowed out it had to be straightened and aligned while heating over a fire. The finished product was kept in a safe, dry place when not in use and became a cherished family possession. One blowgun owned by the Chiltoskey family is said to have been made before the Removal in 1838. Darts for the blowgun were eight to ten inches long, made of locust. The tails of the darts were made of thistledown wound on the staff with a sinew.

Other weapons and tools such as clubs, hoes and axes were fashioned of white oak or hickory wood from young straight trees. Walnut was preferred for gunstocks, however, because of the beauty and richness of the wood.

PERSONAL ADORNMENT

Cherokee women have used the fragrant flowers of sweetshrub to perfume both themselves and their clothing for a long time. Combs were made of rhododendron and sourwood before European contact. Necklaces of continuous five or six foot strands of Job's tears, separated by shell or trade beads, were formerly worn exclusively for medicinal purposes and good luck. Job's tears are the seed of COIX LACRYMA-JOBI. Similar necklaces are available today commercially to satisfy the tourists' demand for souvenirs.

PLANTS IN THE SIXTEENTH CENTURY

The earliest recorded contact between the Cherokees and Europeans took place in 1540. Hernando DeSoto, a Spanish conquistador, led an army through the Cherokee lands during the spring and summer of that year. The information presented here comes primarily from Garcilaso de la Vega's, the FLORIDA OF THE INCA. The accounts of other historians were condensed by James Mooney in MYTHS OF THE CHEROKEES.

DeSoto and his men were searching for gold but they recorded a small amount of information about the Cherokee people and their uses of plants.

beans
PHASEOLUS VULGARIS   FABACEAE
For Food.

cane
ARUNDINARIA GIGANTEA   POACEAE
Burden baskets; dwelling constructed with wooden supports and cane webbing plastered with mud.

corn, maize
ZEA MAYS   POACEAE
For food.

grapes
VITIS SP   VIACEAE
For food.

mulberries
MORUS RUBA   URTICAEAE
For food.

oak
QUERCUS SP.   VITACEAE
For bows.

potatoes
IMPOMOEA PANDURATA   CONVOLVULACEAE
For food.

serviceberries
AMELANCHIER LAEVIS   ROSACEAE
For food.

squash, roman squash
CUCURBITA PEPO   CURCURBITACEAE
For food.

PLANTS EIGHTEENTH-TWENTIETH CENTURY

Twelve lists of plants spanning three centureis are composited in this chapter. The following table presents the sources in their chronological order.

Antoine Bonnefoy	Journal	1741-42
Henry Timberlake	Memoirs	1765
James Adair	History of the American Indian	1775
William Bartram	Travels	1791
Benjamin Barton	Materica medica	1798
Anna Gambold	In Witthoft, 1947	1818
Richard Foreman	Cherokee physician	1846
James Mooney	Myths, Sacred Formulas of the Cherokees	1889-91
J. Mooney & F. Olbrechts	Swimmer Manuscript	1932
William Banks	Ethnobotany of the Cherokee	1953
Edwin Core	Ethnobotany of Southern Indians	1967
Mary U. Chiltoskey	Interviews on the Qualla Boundary	1942-73

Limitations of space have dictated that some of the details of certain uses presented in particular works be left out. We have included common names from these sources, and a small number of translations of Cherokee names. Primary source for scientific names is the MANUAL OF THE VASCULAR FLORA OF THE CAROLINAS: secondary sources includes GRAY'S MANUAL OF BOTANY, 8th edition; or Bailey's MANUAL OF HORTICULTURAL PLANTS. For difficult identification problems we resorted to a combination of the sources listed in th bibliography.

In the list, plants not native are marked Intro. On the right hand side of the page ae some capital letters:

M — medicine   D — dye
F — food   O — other uses

agrimony   M.
AGRIMONIA GYPOSEPALA   ROSACEAE
A. PARVIFLORA
Drink tea of burs to check discharge; to check bowels; for fever; root tea to build up blood; powdered root plus other ingredients for pox; beat up root, form into balls, put in cold water and drink for bowels; root tea to satisfy children's hunger.

alder — red, smooth, tag   M.
ALNUS SERRULATA   BETULACEAE
For pains related to birth; swellings and sprains; skin eruptions; ingredient in tea to clear milky urine; ingredient in tea for menstrual period; an emetic and purgative; rub and blow infusion of bark in eyes for drooping; bark tea for pains; one of six ingredients in steam bath for indigestion or biliousness with swelling of abdomen and yellowish skin; tea for heart trouble; hot berry tea for fever; bark tea **for cough; cold bark scraping tea makes** kidneys act; bark tea to babies for "thrash" a mouth soreness; for toothache, hold tea of bark of alder, white walnut, persimmon, and wild cherry in mouth; drink root tea with virginia pine and dewberry for piles; bathe piles in same tea; cold bark tea to purify blood or bring down high blood pressure; tea with wild cherry, rattlesnake plantain, wild ginger and yellowroot for blood tonic; tea to bath hives.

alder, white   M.
CLETHRA ACUMINATA   CLETHRACEAE
Inner bark is part of drink to vomit disordered bile; hot bark infusion for bowel complaint; decoction of barks of this and wild cherry is drunk to break high fever.

allspice tree, pimento tree M.
PIMENTA DIOICA Intro. LAURACEAE
Stimulant; for lying-in-women who discharges are profuse; for monthly period when discharges are profuse.

aloe, false aloe M.
AGAVE VIRGINICA AMARYLLIDACEAE
STRONG MEDICINE. Chew root for obstinate diarrhea; good for liver; good for worms.

alum-root, american sanicle M.
HEUCHERA AMERICANA SAXIFRAGACEAE
Root is astringent; tea for bowel complaints; immoderate flow of menses; piles and hemorrhages; powdered root on malignant ulcers; tea with honey for thursh or "thrash" and sore mouths; for dysentery; chew root to take coat off tongue; sprinkle tea on bad sores in late summer to heal.

amaranth — green, spring; prince's feather M.
AMARANTH RETROFLEXUS Intro. AMARANTHACEAE
A. SPINOSUS Intro.
A. HYBRIDUS Intro.
Leaves to relieve profuse menstruation; astringent; an ingredient in a green corn medicine.

angelica M.
ANGELICA ATROPURPUREA APIACEAE
Root tonic for ague and fever; cold; obstructed menses; weakly and nervous females; for flatulent colics; gargle for sore throat and mouth.

anise M.
PIMPINELLA ANISUM Intro. APIACEAE
Half a teaspoon in cup of hot water, let stand thirty minutes, drink for catarrh.

apple, sweet M, F, D.
MALUS PUMILA Intro. ROSACEAE
Drink inner bark tea for lost voice; ingredient in cold drink for dry throat of ball players; with carolina vetch and virginia pine to give ball players wind during the game; bark tea for gallstones; piles; food; yellow dye from bark.

arbutus, trailing; ground hog's forehead, mayflower, terrapin's foot M.
EPIGAEA REPENS ERICACEAE
Ingredient for poor digestion; tea for chest ailment; root tea with wintergreen for indigestion; tea for kidneys.

arrowhead M.
SAGITTARIA LATIFOLIA ALISMATACEAE
For baby fevers bathe in a leaf tea, give one sip.

asafoetida M.
FERULA SP. Intro.
Resinous gum from roots for spasms, cramps, flatulence and hysterical affections; whooping cough; asthma; worms; colic.

ash — black, white M.
FRAXINUS NIGRA OLEACEAE
F. AMERICANA
Bark tea to check discharge; tonic of inner bark for liver and stomach.

ash, green -O.
FRAXINUS PENNSYLVANICA OLEACEAE

Handles; ball bats; firewood; lumber; butter paddles.

asparagus   M, F.
ASPARAGUS OFFICINALIS   Intro.   LILIACEAE
Tea for rickets; food.

aster, large blue ; **hardweed,** eyelike   M.
ASTER NOVAE-ANGLIAE   ASTERACEAE
A. LINARIIFOLIUS
Tea for fever; beat up roots to poultice pains; sniff ooze of roots for catarrh; root tea
for diarrhea.

azalea, flame; turkey beard   M, O.
RHODODENDRON CALENDULACEUM   ERICACEAE
Peel and boil a twig, rub on rheumatism; tea for women; fungus "apple" formed on
stem is eaten to appease thirst; flowers to decorate the home.

balm   M.
MELISSA OFFICINALIS   Intro.   LAMIACEAE
Stimulant and tonic; for old colds; typhus fevers; chills and fevers.

balm of gilead, english poplar   M.
POPULUS CANDICANS   Intro.   SALICACEAE
P. NIGRA   Intro.
**Juice of buds on sores; tincture of buds for colic; old bowel complaints; for chronic
rheumatism; old venereal complaints; persons of phlegmatic habits; aching teeth.**

bamboo-brier   M.
SMILAX LAURIFOLIA   LILIACEAE
Root bark astringent and slightly tonic; an ingredient for pox; wash for scalds, burns
and other foul sores.

basswood, linden, lynn tree   M, O.
TILIA AMERICANA   TILIACEAE
T. HETEROPHYLLA
Boil bark, stir cornmeal in ooze to make poultice for boils; inner bark ingredient for
dysentery; chew bark of lightning struck tree, spit on snakebite; inside bark and
twigs for pregnant women for heartburn, weak stomach and bowels; jelly for coughs
and consumption; when stomach has been overheated by too free use of spiritous
liquors; boiled bark twisted into rope; chair bottoms; pulpwood; lumber; carving.

bastard toadflax   M.
COMANDRA UMBELLATA   SANTALACEAE
Steep with roots of pink lady's slipper for kidneys; put juice on cut or sore.

beans — cherry, cornfield, cranberry, jack, lima, october, pinto, pole; butterbeans -F.
PHASEOLUS VULGARIS   FABACEAE
P. LUNATUS   Intro.
Food; bean bread; hickory nut soup.

beans, mole; castor-oil beans   M.
RICINUS COMMUNIS   Intro.   EUPHORBIACEAE
Make poultice of beans to bring boils to a head; drink tea of beans as a purgative.

beans, wild   -F.
APIOS AMERICANA   FABACEAE
Food.

bear-berry, wild cranberry   M, F.
ARCTOSTAPHYLOS UVA-URSI   ERICACEAE
For dropsy and urinary diseases; food.

bear grass   M, O.
YUCCA FILAMENTOSA   LILIACEAE
Tea for diabetes; beaten root with or without tallow for sore salve; to intoxicate fish; ingredient in green corn medicine with broom sedge and spring amaranth; pounded and boiled roots used instead of soap to wash blankets.

beardtongue, hairy   M.
PENSTEMON LAEVIGATUS   SCROPHULARIACEAE
Tea for cramps.

bedstraw, small   M.
GALIUM TRIFLORUM   Intro.   RUBIACEAE
Tea for gallstones.

beech   M, O.
FAGUS GRANDIFOLIA   FAGACEAE
Mast (nuts) chewed for worms; lumber;buttons.

beet   M, F.
BETA VULGARIS   Intro.   CHENOPODIACEAE
Poultice boils with wilted leaves; food.

beggar lice   M, O.
HACKELIA VIRGINIA   BORAGINACEAE
Decoction for kidney trouble; bruised root with bear oil is ointment for cancer; roots are part of decoction given for itch; for good memory; love charms.

bellflowers, tsu-hi-tsu-gi, wild oats   M, F.
UVULARIA SESSILIFOLIA   LILIACEAE
Root steep for diarrhea; poultice boil; eat as cooked greens.

benne plant   M.
SESAMUM INDICUM   Intro.   PEDALIACEAE
Decoction of leaves and seeds for flux, dystentery and cholera-infantum; seed oil is cathartic.

birch — cherry, mountain, red, river, sweet   M.
BETULA LENTA   BETULACEAE
B. NIGRA
Bark tea for milky urine; chew leaves or drink tea for dysentery; tea for colds; bark infusion for stomach.

birch, yellow; mountain mahogany   -O.
BETULA LUTEA   BETULACEAE
Lumber.

bittersweet   M.
CELASTRUS SCANDENS   CELASTRACEAE
Bark tea to settle stomach; chew root for cough; leaves are highly astringent; decoction for bowel complaint; wash for foul ulcers; strong tea combined with red raspberry leaves for pains of childbirth; scratch rheumatism with thorny branch.

blackberry — allegheny, high bush; dewberry   M, F.

RUBUS ALLEGHENIENSIS   ROSACEAE
R. ARGUTUS
R. TRIVIALIS
R. FLAGELLARIS
Ingredient in decoction to regulate urination; root or leaf tea to check bowels; astringent and tonic; venereal disease; weakly phlegmatic persons; sweeten with honey to wash sore throat; chew washed root to take coat off tongue; root tea with virginia pine and alder drunk and used as wash for piles; tea for rheumatism; juice and fruit for food.

blackgum   M.
NYSSA SYLVATICA   NYSSACEAE
An ingredient for worms; inner bark is part of drink to vomit bile; ingredient in drink for milky urine; ingredient in decoction for diarrhea; bark tea with heart's-a-bustin-with-love, grape, sweetgum, sycamore, beech and sawbrier for "bad disease"; drip strong root ooze into eyes; bark tea for flooding; tea for childbirth.

black heart, lady's thumb   M.
POLYGONUM PERSICARIA   Intro.   POLYGONACEAE
Crush leaves and rub on poison ivy; drink tea for gravel; boil and mix tea with meal to poultice pain.

blood leather, rock tripe   M.
GYROPHORA DILLENII   GYROPHORACEAE
Stop bleeding from open wounds.

blood root, red puccoon, red root   M, D.
SANGUINARIA CANADENSIS   PAPAVERACEAE
Decoction of root in small doses for coughs, lung inflammations and croup; wash for ulcers and sores; steep in vinegar for tetterworm; snuff for polypus; pulverize root and sniff for catarrh; tea with broom sedge for cough; red dye.

bluebells, lungwort, virginia cowslip   M.
MERTENSIA VIRGINICA   BORAGINACEAE
For whooping cough; consumption.

bluets   M.
HOUSTONIA CAERULEA   RUBIACEAE
Tea to stop bedwetting.

blue-eyed grass   M, F.
SISYRINCHIUM AUGUSTIFOLIUM   IRIDACEAE
Root steep for childrens diarrhea; eaten as cooked greens to keep regular.

boneset, indian sage, thorough-stem, throughwort   M.
EUPATORIUM PERFOLIATUM   ASTERACEAE
Tonic; sudorific; stimulant; emetic; purgative; antiseptic; diuretic; for fever; biliary system and ague; tea for colds, sore throat, flu.

bouncing bet, lady's washbowl   M, O.
SAPONARIA OFFICINALIS   Intro.   CARYOPHYLLACEAE
Poultice boils; use as soap.

branch lettuce, saxifrage   M, F.
SAXIFRAGA PENSYLVANICA   SAXIFRAGACEAE
Root poultice for sore swollen muscles, eaten as raw greens.

broom sedge   M, D.
ANDROPOGON VIRGINICUS   POACEAE
Tea for frost bite; ingredient in green corn medicine; bathe itch in ooze; mix tea with
tallow for sores; make tea to check bowels; stems, alone or with onion peels, make a
yellow dye.

buckeye, red   M, O.
AESCULUS PAVIA   HIPPOCASTANACEAE
Pounded nuts are poultice for white swelling, sprains, tumors and infections;
ingredient in drink for dyspepsia from overeating; drink steep of ground nut meat to
prevent fainting; bark tea drunk to facilitate delivery; cold bark infusion with
chestnut given to stop bleeding after delivery; small pieces of nut chewed and
swallowed for colic; salve for sores; carry nut in pocket for piles, rheumatism and
good luck.

buckeye — sweet, yellow   -O.
AESCULUS OCTANDRA   HIPPOCASTANACEAE
Carving, lumber; pulpwood; dough trays; baby cradles; masks.

buckthorn   M.
RHAMNUS CATHARTICUS   Intro.   RHAMNACEAE
Bark and fruit powerful cathartic; decoction of bark for itch; to wash sore and
inflamed eyes.

buffalo nut, colic ball, oilnut   M.
PYRULARIA PUBERA   SANTALACEAE
Salve for old sores; chew nut to make vomit for colic.

bulrush, great   M.
SCIRPUS VALIDUS   CYPERACEAE
Decoction as emetic; ingredient in medicine for spoiled saliva.

burdock   M.
ARCTIUM LAPPA   Intro.   ASTERACEAE
Root or seed tea for cleansing blood; venereal; rheumatism; gravel; scurvy and
weakly females.

burdock, common   M.
ARCTIUM MINUS   ASTERACEAE
Boil to make ooze for leg ulcers; bathe swollen legs.

butterfly weed, chigger weed, flux weed, pleurisy-root, witch weed   M, O.
ASCLEPIAS TUBEROSA   ASCLEPIADACEAE
Seeds or root are a gentle laxative; boil seeds in new milk for diarrhea; expectorant;
for pleurisy; pains in the breast, stomach and intestine and for inflammation of
lungs; tea for bloody flux; root tea for heart trouble; stems for belts.

button snakeroot, rattlesnake master   M.
ERYNGIUM YUCCIFOLIUM   APIACEAE
Remedy for snakebites; decoction to prevent whooping cough; hold tea in mouth for
toothaches.

button snake-root   M.
LIATRIS SPICATA   ASTERACEAE
Root is warming stimulant; diuretic; sudorific; expectorant; carminative; anodyne;
decoction or tincture for colic, back-ache, pain in limbs; dropsy.

cabbage   M, F.
BRASSICA OLERACEA   Intro.   BRASSICACEAE
Wilt leaf to poultice boil; food.

calamus, rush, sweet flag   M.
ACORUS CALAMUS   Intro.   ARACEAE
Possesses stimulant and stomachic virtues; good for flatulent colic; white swelling;
worms; yellowish urine; diuretic; diaphoretic; for dropsy; gravel; root chewed for
colds, headache, sore throat; drink hot root tea for colds; chew root and swallow juice
to check bowels; drink tea to prevent recurrent spasms.

camphor tree   M.
CINNAMOMUM CAMPHORA   Intro.   LAURACEAE
Sweating medicine for colds, winter fevers; good for hysterical females with nervous
diseases and headaches; stimulant in sickness and fainting; anodyne in colic and
cramp; worms.

cane — river, switch   -O.
ARUNDINARIA GIGANTEA   POACEAE
Fuel; candles; arrowshafts; blowgun used with darts for small game; baskets; used
as knives as last resort in committing suicide in 1738 small pox epidemic; "joint of
reed" used for making flutes.

cardinal flower — blue   M.
LOBELIA CARDINALIS   CAMPANULACEAE
L. SIPHILITICA
Root tea for stomach trouble; root tea for worms; ingredient in drink for pain; leaf
tea to reduce fever; snuff cold tea for nose bleed; tea for rheumatism; poultice of
crushed leaves for headache; warm leaf tea for colds; root poultice for risings; tea
for sores hard to heal; croup; syphilis.

catnip, cat eats   M.
NEPETA CATARIA   Intro.   LAMIACEAE
Tea for female obstructions; hysterics; worms; spasms; colic; poultice swellings;
syrup with honey for coughs and colds; tea for babies' colds; tea for hives; leaf
poultice for boils; leaf tea is stimulant and tonic; tea for fevers; tea of leaves for
stomach.

cedar, red   M, O.
JUNIPERUS VIRGINIANA   CUPRESSACEAE
Diaphoretic; tea for colds; female obstructions; measles; berries boiled in sweet
milk for worms; ointment for itch and cutaneous diseases; white swelling;
rheumatism; carving; furniture; fence posts; moth proofing.

chamomile   M.
ANTHEMIS NOBILIS   **Intro.**   ASTERACEAE
Strong tea of flower or herb for female obstructions and hysterical affections; colic;
vomiting; bowel complaints; poultice for ulcers and hard swellings.

cherry — bird, fire, wild black, wild red; **chokecherry**   M, F, O.
PRUNUS CERASUS   ROSACEAE
P. PENSYLVANICA
P. SEROTINA
P. VIRGINIANA
Bark tea for fever; fresh bark decoction for the "great chill", ague; warm tea at first
pains of labor; bark decoction with white alder to break fever; bark tea for cough and

colds; with barks of spicewood and flowering dogwood added to corn whiskey to break out measles; with alder, rattlesnake plantain, wild ginger and yellowroot makes a blood tonic; bark tea for "thrash"; decoction of inner bark for lost voice; one of six ingredients in steam bath for indigestion or biliousness with swelling abdomen and yellowish skin; astringent; bark of root makes wash for old sores and ulcers; boil fruit for blood discharged from bowels; fruit for food; carving; lumber; furniture.

chestnut   M, F, D, O.
CASTANEA DENTATA   FAGACEAE
"In July, half boil chestnuts and take off the rind. Slice rows of corn and pound in a large wooden mortar which is wider at the top than at the bottom. Knead both together, then wrap them up in a green cornblade, about an inch thick, and boil well..." (James Adair) tea of year old leaves for heart trouble; leaves from young sprouts cure old sores; cold bark tea with buckeye to stop bleeding after birth; apply warmed galls to make infant's navel recede; boil leaves with mullein and brown sugar for cough syrup; dip leaves in hot water and put on sores; tea for typhoid; for stomach; bark makes brown dye; firewood (pops badly); lumber (wormy or good); rails for fences; acid wood; coffee substitute (parched).

chicory   M.
CICHORIUM INTYBUS   Intro.   ASTERACEAE
Root tea is tonic for nerves.

chickweed, common   M.
CERASTIUM HOLOSTEOIDES   Intro.   CARYOPHYLLACEAE
Stem and root tea with yellow lady's slipper for worms in children.

chinaberry, china tree   M, O.
MELIA AZEDARACH   Intro.   MELIACEAE
Root and bark tea for worms; scald-head; ringworm; tetterworm; crush leaves to drive out house insects.

chinquapin   M.
CASTANEA PUMILA   FAGACEAE
For fever blisters; heat brittle leaves and blow on patient to relieve headaches; chills and cold sweats.

cinnamon tree   M.
CINNAMOMUM ZEYLANICUM   Intro.   LAURACEAE
Bark tea for flu; stimulant; stomachic; tonic; carminative; for latter stages of pregnancy; strengthens mother and child; to stop flooding before and after delivery.

cinquefoil, five finger   M.
PONTENTILLA SIMPLEX   ROSACEAE
Root tea mouthwash to cure "thrash"; root is astringent; for fevers and acute diseases with great debility; dysentery; ball players ate root and bathed in root tea to prevent injury and for wind.

clover — red, white   M.
TRIFOLIUM PRATENSE   **Intro.**   FABACEAE
T. REPENS   Intro.
Tea for fevers; "Brights disease"; leucorrhea.

cocklebur   M.
XANTHIUM SPINOSUM   Intro.   ASTERACEAE
Bur tea to unstick object in throat; for cramps; chew roots for rattlesnake bite; root

tea is emetic; tea for croup.

cohosh, black; black snakeroot, rattleweed   M.
CIMICIFUGA RACEMOSA   RANUNCULACEAE
Roots in alcoholic spirits for rheumatism; tonic; diuretic; anodyne; emmenagogue; slightly astringent; tea for colds; coughs; consumptions; constipation; tea for rheumatism; fatigue; hives; to make baby sleep; backache.

cohosh, blue; blue-**berry, papoose root**   M.
CAULOPHYLLUM THALICTROIDES   BERBERIDACEAE
Root decoction or syrup, for fits, hysterics; colics and nerves; promotes child-birth; allays inflammation and prevents mortification of womb; root for rheumatism; hold root ooze in mouth for toothache; rub leaves on oak-poison.

columbine   M.
AQUILEGIA CANADENSIS   RANUNCULACEAE
Tea for heart trouble; cold tea to stop flux.

columbo root   M.
SWERTIA CAROLINIENSIS   GENTIANACEAE
Root for tonic; for indigestion and dysentery; to check vomiting; for colics; cramps; want of appetite; antiseptic.

comfrey   M.
SYMPHYTUM OFFICINALE   Intro.   BORAGINACEAE
Mild tea for flooding after childbirth; for flux or dysentery; roots in water for gonorrhea; for pregnant women with heartburn costiveness; for sprains and bruises.

comfrey, wild; beggar lice   M.
GYNOGLOSSUM VIRGINIANUM   BORAGINACEAE
Roots are part of decoction given for itch; ingredient in green corn medicine; root syrup for milky urine; root for cancer; take this and other "stick-on" plants, drink decoction every four days for bad memory.

coneflower, green-headed; **so-cha-ni**   -F.
RUDBECKIA LACINIATA   ASTERACEAE
Use as cooked spring salad to keep well.

coneflower, black-eyed susan, deer-eye daisy, a-wi-a-ka-ta   M, D.
RUDBECKIA FULGIDA   ASTERACEAE
R. HIRTA
Root ooze for earache; bathe sores in warm root tea; root tea drunk for flux and some private diseases; wash for snakebites and swelling caused by worms; tea for dropsy; brown dye.

corn, maize, se-lu   M, F, O.
ZEA MAYS   POACEAE
Eat parched grains for long wind; tea of silks for gravel; food, salve of smut; shucks for dolls.

corn salad   -F.
VALERIANELLA OLITORIA   VALERIANACEAE
Cooked greens.

cornel, stiff   M.
CORNUS STRICTA   CORNACEAE

Tea for lost voice.

couch grass, dog grass, quack grass   M.
AGROPYRON REPENS   Intro.   POACEAE
Boil to wash swollen legs; tea for gravel; tea for continence and bedwetting.

cowbane, spotted; musquash root, poison hemlock, water hemlock   M, O.
CICUTA MACULATA   APIACEAE
SUICIDE TO EAT LARGE QUANTITIES. Chew and swallow roots for four consecutive days to become sterile forever; old timers used this to find out how long they would live, if they got dizzy chewing the roots they would die soon, if not they would live a long time; corn is soaked in a root tea before planting to repel insect pests.

crabapple   M, F.
MALUS CORONARIA   ROSACEAE
Drink bark tea for gallstones; piles; tea to wash sore mouth; food.

creases   -F.
BARBAREA VULGARIS   Intro.   BRASSICACEAE
Eat as cooked salad to purify blood.

cross vine   M.
ANISOSTICHUS CAPREOLATA   BIGNONIACEAE
Leaf tea to cleanse blood.

crowfoot — small-flowered, hooked; buttercup   M, F.
RANUNCULUS ABORTIVUS   RANUNCULACEAE
R. ACRIS   Intro.
R. RECURVATUS
Tea gargle for sore throat; juice used as sedative; tea for "thrash"; poultice abscesses; cooked greens.

culver's root, culver's physic, bowman's root   M.
VERONICASTRUM VIRGINICUM   SCROPHULARIACEAE
Purgative; good for typhus and bilious fevers; root is diaphoretic; tonic; antiseptic; for inactive liver with indian physic and boneset; chew for colic; tea for backache.

dandelion   M.
TARAXACUM OFFICINALE   Intro.   ASTERACEAE
Root tea for blood; chew for toothache; tea of herb to calm nerves.

dandelion, goat   M.
PYRRHOPAPPUS CAROLINIANUS   ASTERACEAE
Drink tea to purify blood.

devil's shoestring, catgut; goat's rue   M.
TEPHROSIA VIRGINIANA   FABACEAE
Decoction for lassitude; women wash their hair in decoction of roots to prevent breaking or falling out; ball players rub on limbs to toughen them; root tea given to child to make it strong and muscular; ingredient in medicine for kidney trouble; tea for worms.

devil's walkingstick, hercules' club, prickly ash, prickly elder   M.
ARALIA SPINOSA   FABACEAE
Tea of roasted and pounded roots as strong emetic; tonic; diaphoretic and

carminative; rheumatism; venereal diseases; flatulent colic; ache of decaying teeth; salve of the roots for old sores; bathe in root ooze for paralysis.

dittany, mountain ditney   M.
CUNILA ORIGANOIDES   LAMIACEAE
Tea for colds; headaches; fevers; to increase **perspiration**; tonic; stimulant; snake-bite; strong tea to increase labor pains and facilitate childbirth.

dock — curly, patience   M.
RUMEX CRISPUS   Intro.   POLYGONACEAE
R. PATIENTIA   Intro.
Root tea to correct fluids; bruised root tea for poultice of old sores, ulcers and hard tumors; salve for eruptions and itch of skin; tea for dysentery and bowel complaints; juice for ringworm or tetterworm; drink root tea for blood; rub leaves in mouth for sore throat; feed beaten roots to horse with sick stomach; root tea for constipation.

dodder, common; love-in-a-tangle   M.
CUSCUTA GRONOVII   CONVOLVULACEAE
Poultice for bruises.

dogbane, spreading   M.
APOCYNUM ANDROSAEMIFOLIUM   APOCYNACEAE
Bathe dogs for mange.

dog-fennel, mayweed, wild camomile   M.
ANTHEMIS COTULA   Intro.   ASTERACEAE
Emetic; tonic; sudorific and anodyne for colds; hysterics; epilepsy; dropsy; asthma; rheumatism; fevers; bruised herb applied externally draws blister.

dog hobble, gray fetter brush   M.
LEUCOTHOE AXILLARIS   ERICACEAE
Warm infusion for shifting pains; warm infusion rubbed on to cure rheumatism, languor; leaf decoction with mountain laurel and large rhododendron for rheumatism; apply root ooze to mangy dog; bath itch in tea of leaf and stem.

dogwood — alternate-leaf, blue, flowering   M, O.
CORNUS ALTERNIFOLIA   CORNACEAE
C. FLORIDA
Bark tea for women's backache; bark of root for poultice; bark of root is tonic, stimulant, antiseptic, astringent and for intermittent fevers; flower tea for colic; bark and root is one ingredient in tea for childhood diseases like worms, measles, and chicken pox; ingredient in tea for diarrhea; drink tea of inner bark for lost voice; bark tea of dogwood, wild cherry, and spicewood, added to corn whiskey, drunk to break out measles; bark chewed for headache; bathe in tea of beaten bark for poisons of any kind; tea of flowers to sweat off flu; ooze of bark to poultice ulcer; tea for blood; carving; shuttles for looms.

dutchman's pipe vine, black sarsaparilla   M.
ARISTOLOCHIA MACROPHYLLA   ARISTOLOCHIACEAE
Root decoction externally for swelling of feet and legs; stalk chips is an ingredient in tea for yellowish urine.

dwarf-bay, mezeron   M.
DAPHNE MEZEREUM   Intro.   THYMELAEACEAE
Highly stimulant and diaphoretic; bark of root for last stages of the venereal to relieve nocturnal pains and remove venereal nodes.

earth star, puffball   M.
GEASTER HYGROMETRICUS   LYCOPERDALES
Dust snuff on baby's navel to cause quick healing.

elder — american, sweet, white   M, F.
SAMBUCUS CANADENSIS   CAPRIFOLIACEAE
S. NIGRA   Intro.
Diuretic; cathartic; emetic; for dropsy; light sickness among children; salve for
burns and eruptions of the skin; decoction for summer complaint; berry tea, for
rheumatism; berry or flower tea is tonic for boils; wash sores with leaves to keep
down infection; drink tea of flowers to sweat out fever; berries in jellies and other
foods.

elecampane   M.
INULA HELENIUM   Intro.   ASTERACEAE
Root for lung disorders; coughts; asthmas; consumption; for female obstructions
and pregnant women with weak bowels and wombs.

elm — red, slippery   M, O.
ULMUS RUBRA   ULMACEAE
Inside bark to poultice old sores, burns and wounds; internally soothes stomach and
bowels; mild laxative; for pregnant women with heartburn, dysentery and chronic
bowel complaints; for quinsies, colds, coughs, catarrhs, consumptions and breast
complaints; boil bark to wash eyes; chew inner bark and spit on baseball glove,
makes the ball stick to the glove.

evening primrose, hog weed   M, F.
OENOTHERA BIENNIS   Intro.   ONAGRACEAE
Tea for overfatness; hot root poultice for piles; cooked greens when young.

fennel, sweet   M.
FOENICULUM VULGARE   Intro.   APIACEAE
Tonic; colic; child's flatulent colic; given to women in labor; for colds.

fern, bladder   M.
CYSTOPTERIS PROTRUSA   Intro.   ASPIDIACEAE
Ingredient in tea for chills.

fern, bracken; cholera-morbus root   M.
PTERIDIUM AQUILINUM   PTERIDACEAE
Root tonic; antiseptic; antiemetic; for cholera-morbus.

fern — christmas, shield; bear's bed   M., F.
POLYSTICHUM ACROSTICHOIDES   ASPIDIACEAE
Roots an ingredient in an emetic, ingredient in medicine rubbed on skin for
rheumatism after scratching; ingredient in decoction for toothache; ingredient in
decoction for chills; cold root infusion for stomach ache or bowel complaint; tea for
rheumatism, fever and pneumonia; fiddle heads for food.

fern, cinnamon; fern-snake-root   M., F.
OSMUNDA CINNAMOMEA   OSMUNDACEAE
For snake bites, chew root, swallow a portion and apply the rest to the wound, repeat
as necessary; roots are ingredient for rheumatism; ingredient in decoction for chills;
eat cooked fronds as spring tonic.

fern, hay-scented   M.

DENNSTAEDTIA PUNCTILOBULA   PTERIDACEAE
Ingredient in tea for chills.

fern, maiden; maidenhair spleenwort, maidenhair   M.
ASPLENIUM TRICHOMANES   ASPLENIACEAE
Tea for coughs; diseases of breast; acrid humors; irregular menses; liver
complaints.

fern, maiden-hair   M.
ADIANTUM PEDATUM   PTERIDACEAE
Tea of whole plant used as an emetic in case of ague and fever; STRONG
MEDICINE; poultice for rheumatism and chills; tea for rheumatism; chills and
fever; smoke powdered leaves for heart trouble; steep of entire plant is blown over
head and chest of patient where he is hot; for sudden paralytic attacks as in bad
pneumonia of children; powder and snuff for asthma; powder and smoke for asthma.

fern, male   M.
DRYOPTERIS FILIX-MAS   POLYPODIACEAE
Drink root tea for worms.

fern, rattlesnake   M.
BOTRYCHIUM VIRGINIANUM   OPHIOGLOSSACEAE
Boil root down to syrup and rub on snake bite.

fern, wood   M.
DRYOPTERIS MARGINALIS   POLYPODIACEAE
Root tea is emetic; with or without other ingredients used for rheumatism; hold
warm tea in mouth for toothache.

feverfew   M.
CHRYSANTHEMUM PARTHENIUM   Intro.   ASTERACEAE
Bathe swollen feet in tea.

fir, balsam; silver fir of america   M.
ABIES FRASERI   PINACEAE
Balsam for breast and lung complaints with pain, soreness or cough; for females with
"whites"; falling of the womb and weak backs; for venereal and urinary diseases; to
loosen bowels and cleanse and heal internal ulcers; for wounds and ulcers; burst
blister, take ooze for kidney trouble; put two drops of turpentine with blister to flush
kidney.

flax   M.
LINUM USITATISSIMUM   Intro.   LINACEAE
Seeds for gravel or burning in passing water; for violent colds, coughs, and diseases
of lungs; pour decoction over body to cure fever attacks.

fly-poison   M, O.
AMIANTHIUM MUSCAETOXICUM   LILIACEAE
For itch; crow poison.

foamflower   M.
TIARELLA CORDIFOLIA   SAXIFRAGACEAE
Tea held in mouth to remove white coat from tongue.

four-o'clock, pretty by night   M, O.
MIRABILIS NYCTAGINEA   NYCTAGINACEAE

Beat root to poultice boils; milk poured over the leaves becomes fly-poison.

foxglove — yellow false, fern leaf false, smooth false   M.
AUREOLARIA FLAVA   SCROPHULARIACEAE
A. PEDICULARIA
A. LAEVIGATA
Infusion drunk while fasting for four days for apoplexy; ingredient in decoction for dysentery.

frost-root, skervish, poor robin's plantain   M.
ERIGERON PHILADELPHICUS   ASTERACEAE
E. PULCHELLUS
Astringent; diuretic; sudorific; gout; suppressed menstruation; coughs; hemorrhages; dimness of sight; tea for kidneys; for spitting of blood; epilepsy; poultice for headache; cold root tea, or chewed root for colds; mix boiled plant with tallow to use on sores.

frostweed   M.
HELIANTHEMUM CANADENSE   CISTACEAE
Leaf steep drank for kidneys.

galax, beetleweed, colt's foot   M.
GALAX APHYLLA   DIAPENSIACEAE
Root tea for kidney trouble; tea for nerves.

gall of the earth, lions foot   M, F.
PRENANTHES TRIFOLIOLATA   ASTERACEAE
P. SERPENTARIA
Roots are ingredient in stomach-ache medicine; eat as cooked salad.

garlic — field, wild   M.
ALLIUM SATIVUM   Intro.   LILIACEAE
A. VINEALE   **Intro.**
A. CANADENSE
Stimulant; carminative; diuretic; expectorant; a mild cathartic; useful for scurvy; dropsy; asthma; removes deafness; tincture prevents worms and colic in children; fry and put on chest for croup.

gentian   M.
GENTIANA QUINQUEFOLIA   GENTIANACEAE
Root tonic; stimulant and cathartic; laxative; remedy for weak stomach and hysterical affections; for dyspepsy.

geranium, wild; cranesbill, mountain alum   M.
GERANIUM MACULATUM   GERANIACEAE
Used for open wounds; astringent; styptic; decoction with fox grapes to wash children's mouths in thrush; removes canker sores.

ginger   M.
ZINGIBER OFFICINALE   Intro.   ZINGIBERACEAE
Use tea for flu; good in tea for colds and colics; good for monthly period; for lying-in-women; weak tea for infants for hives or colic; good for looseness or weakness of bowels or intestines; ingredient in stimulating poultices; chew for relief of heartburn in pregnant women;

ginger, wild; heart-leaves, heart snakeroot   M., O.

ASARUM CANADENSE   ARISTOLOCHIACEAE
Fresh leaves applied to wounds; root is stimulant (powerful); colds; coughs; female obstructions; for scant or painful menstruation; worms; snuff of dried leaves for head and eyes; leaves, roots or blossoms, for hysterical or nervous debility; typhus fever; ague and fever; colds; coughs; ingredient in cure for swollen breasts; ingredient in tea for poor digestion; make root tea with rattlesnake plantain, alder, wild cherry and yellowroot for blood; drink tea to start periods; liquid or salve for sores; tea for flux; root tea for heart trouble; dried leaves pounded for snuff.

gingseng, ginseng, snag   M.
PANAX QUINQUEFOLIUM   ARALIACEAE
Root tonic; expectorant; weakness of the womb and nervous affections; convulsions; palsy; vertigo; dysentery; headache; chew root for colic; tea for thrush; Cherokees sold large quantities of "sang" to traders in late 19th century for 50 cents a pound, nearly two day's wages (James Mooney).

ginseng, dwarf; white sarsaparilla   M.
PANAX TRIFOLIUM   ARALIACEAE
"a root which never fails curing the most inveterate venereal disease" (Henry Timberlake); for nervous debility; dropsy; gout; scrofulous sores; rheumatism; diseases induced by mercury; pox; dyspepsia; liver; apoplexy; ingredient to relieve sharp pains in the breast; with other ingredients, tea for bold hives, a children's disease that will bring death in two or three hours; chew root for short breath; cough; chew root for colic, or make hot water infusion; beat the roots with trout lily in cold infusion for fainting; tea for tuberculosis.

globe flower, spreading   M.
TROLLIUS LAXUS   Intro.   RANUNCULACEAE
Steep leaves and stem in boiling water for "thrash".

goat's beard   M.
ARUNCUS DIOICUS   Intro.   ROSACEAE
Tea to stop excessive urination; beat root and apply for bee stings in eye or face; infusion of root to bathe swollen feet; hot root tea to keep from losing too much blood at childbirth, will relieve suffering.

goldenrod   M.
SOLIDAGO ODORA   ASTERACEAE
Tea for fever; for colds and coughs; diaphoretic; tonic; stimulant; nerves; measles; female obstructions; steep and drink for bloody discharge from bowels; roots of two goldenrods are used in tea for summer complaint; hold root tea in mouth for neuralgia; chew root for sore mouth; leaf tea for tuberculosis.

golden seal, yellowroot   M, D.
HYDRASTIS CANADENSIS   RANUNCULACEAE
Cancer; tonic; for general debility; improve appetite; dyspepsy; bath for local inflammations; dye.

gooseberry   M.
RIBES ROTUNDIFOLIUM   SAXIFRAGACEAE
Tea for measles; bark tea to check bowels; leaf tea for nerves.

goosegrass   M.
GALIUM APARINE   RUBIACEAE
Tea to move bowels.

gourd, bottlegourd, rattlegourd   M, F, O.
LAGENARIA VULGARIS   CUCURBITACEAE
Soak seeds and poutice boil; eaten by some; dippers; ceremonial rattles.

grape — fox, frost, summer   M., F.
VITIS LABRUSCA   VITACEAE
V. VULPINA
V. AESTIVALIS
Wilt leaves to draw **soreness** from breast after birth of child; leaf tea for liver;
ingredient for diarrhea; ingredient for irregular urination; bark tea with
hearts-a-bustin'-with-love, sweetgum, sycamore, american beech, sawbrier and
black gum for "bad disease"; drink for fall tonic; leaf tea for blood; tea for stomach;
decoction with wood geranium to wash children's mouth in thrush; food.

greenbrier, common; carrion **flower, sawbrier.**   M, F.
SMILAX ROTUNDIFOLIA   LILIACEAE
S. TAMNIFOLIA
S. HERBACEA
S. GLAUCA
Root decoction with sycamore and carolina hemlock to aid in expelling afterbirth; for
rheumatism; scratch with brier and rub medicine in scratches for local pains,
muscular cramps and twitching; bark tea with hearts-a-bustin-with-love, sweetgum,
summer grape, sycamore, american beech and black gum for "bad disease"; powder
and beat up leaves to put on galled places; parch and powder for scalds; wilt leaves to
put on boils; tea for stomach trouble; roots for food.

ground cherry, little tomato   -F.
PHYSALIS HETEROPHYLLA   SOLANACEAE
Edible berry.

ground ivy   M.
GLECOMA HEDERACEAE   Intro.   LAMIACEAE
Tea for babies' hives; tea for measles; tea for colds.

harebell, southern   M.
CAMPANULA DIVARICATA   CAMPANULACEAE
Root tea for diarrhea.

hawkweed, rabbit's ear   M.
HIERACIUM VENOSUM   ASTERACEAE
Root tea with partridgeberry for bowel complaints.

hawthorn, little hip   M.
CRATAEGUS SPATHULATA   ROSACEAE
Bark tea to give good circulation; bark tea drunk or bathed in by ball players to ward
off tacklers; bark tea to prevent current spasms; eat berries for appetite.

hazelnut   **M,F.**
CORYLUS AMERICANA   BETULACEAE
Inner bark used as part of drink to vomit bile; scrape off bark, soak in water, drink for
hives; nuts for food.

heart leaf, virginia tea root   M.
HEXASTYLIS VIRGINICA   ARISTOLOCHIACEAE
Drink tea to stop blood from passing.

hearts-a-bustin'-with-love, cats paw, strawberry bush, wahoo   M.
EUONYMUS AMERICANUS   CELASTRACEAE
Tonic; astringent; antiseptic; expectorant; for breast complaints; spitting blood; for white swelling in first stage; ingredient in decoction for irregular urination; ingredient in tea for "bad disease" with sweetgum, summer grape, sycamore, american beech, sawbrier and black gum; drink root steep for claps; warm tea for stomach ache; drink root tea for falling of the womb; rub on bark tea for cramps in veins; sniff bark tea for sinus.

hemlock   M, D, O.
TSUGA CANADENSE   PINACEAE
T. CAROLINIANA
Tea of stems tips used for kidneys; bark poultice for itching armpits; roots used in decoction to aid in expelling afterbirth with sycamore and sawbrier; chew root to check bowels; bark makes rosy-tan dye; lumber; firewood (pops badly); bark for tanic acid; pulpwood; inner bark for basketry.

hemp, indian   M, O.
APOCYNUM CANNABINUM   APOCYNACEAE
Root for pox; for dropsy and uterine obstructions; rheumatism; asthma and coughs; whooping cough; root tea for kidneys (Brights disease); used for cords; fibers were used to weave grave cloth material.

hepatica, liverwort   M.
HEPATICA ACUTILOBA   RANUNCULACEAE
Ingredient in cure for swollen breasts; ingredient in decoction for poor digestion; tea for liver; laxative.

hickory — mockernut, pale, shell-bark, white, white-heart   M, F, O.
CARYA TOMENTOSA   JUGLANDACEAE
C. LACINIOSA
C. PALLIDA
Diaphoretic; for bile; to invigorate stomach; large dose as emetic; for cold; female obstructions; bark steep drunk by ball players to make limbs supple; for relief of pain of poliomyelitis; chew bark for sore mouth; inner bark is astringent and detergent; dressings for cuts, ruptured or cut blood vessels; food; blowgun darts; arrow shafts; handles for tools; firewood; barrel hoops; corn beaters; inner bark for chair bottoms; for finishing baskets.

hoarhound, wild   M.
EUPATORIUM PILOSUM   ASTERACEAE
Tonic; for breast complaints; colds; phthisics; laxative; increases urination.

hog peanut   M, F.
AMPHICARPA BRACTEATA   FABACEAE
Blow root tea on snakebite wound; root tea for diarrhea; roots for food.

holly, american   M, D, O.
ILEX OPACA   AQUIFOLIACEAE
Berries for colics; scratch cramped muscles with leaves; chew berries for dyspepsia; berries in dye; wood for spoons; carving; Christmas trees (fifty years ago).

honeysuckle vine, japanese   -O.
LONICERA JAPONICA   Intro.   CAPRIFOLIACEAE
Vines for baskets.

hophornbeam, eastern; ironwood   M.
OSTRYA VIRGINIANA   BETULACEAE
Hold hot bark tea with cucumber tree tea in mouth for toothache; boil bark to bathe
sore muscles; bark tea to build up blood.

hop vine   M.
HUMULUS LUPULUS   CANNABACEAE
For gravel; inflamed kidneys and bladder; alleviates pain and produces sleep; for
rheumatism; breast and female complaints where womb is debilitated; for falling of
the womb.

horehound — water, white   M.
MARRUBIUM VULGARE   Intro.   LAMIACEAE
For hoarseness; coughs; colds; and breast complaints; tea for babies; make cough
syrup with sugar.

horehound — water, wild   M.
LYCOPUS VIRGINICUS   LAMIACEAE
Chew root for snakebites, swallow a portion and apply the rest to the wound; tea
drunk at green corn ceremony; chewed root given to infants to give them eloquence of
speech; wring plant in sweet milk, boil, and feed to snakebitten dog.

hornbeam, american; blue beech, ironwood, water beech   M.
CARPINUS CAROLINIANA   BETULACEAE
Inner bark is astringent; ingredient in tea for flux; drink for a mild form of navel
yellowness; drink for cloudy urine.

horse gentian, feverwort   M.
TRIOSTEUM PERFOLIATUM   CAPRIFOLIACEAE
Emetic and febrifuge; soak sore feet in tea; bathe in ooze for leg swelling.

horsemint — blue, red; bee-balm, wild bergamot, oswego tea   M, F.
MONARDA DIDYMA   LAMIACEAE
M. FISTULOSA
Leaf poultice for headache; used for colds; leaf and top tea for weak bowels and
stomach; diuretic; diaphoretic; for colds and female obstructions; carminative for
colic; flatulency; hysterics; leaf or root infusion drunk and wiped on head for
nosebleed; hot leaf tea to bring out measles; tea to sweat off flu; tea for heart trouble;
warm poultice for headache; tea for fever; for restful sleep; food.

horseradish   M.
ARMORACIA RUSTICANA   Intro.   BRASSICACEAE
Diuretic; tonic; for gravel; increases appetite; aids digestion; for rheumatism;
asthma; colds; obstructed menses; chew on roots for diseases of the tongue and
mouth; gargle with tea for sore throat.

horsetail grass   M.
EQUISETUM ARVENSE   EQUISETACEAE
E. HYEMALE
Tea for kidneys; strong tea for constipation.

huckleberry   M, F.
GAYLUSSACIA BACCATA   ERICACEAE
Tea of leaves for Bright's disease; leaf tea for dysentery; bark tea to check bowels;
food.

hyssop   M.
HYSSOPUS OFFICINALIS   Intro.   LAMIACEAE
Syrup for colds; coughs; asthma and other lung and breast diseases; tea for fevers;
to bring on menses.

indian cucumber, wild cucumber   M.
ECHINOCYSTIS LOBATA   CUCURBITACEAE
Rheumatism; chills and fevers; obstructed menses; tea for kidneys.

indian paintbrush   -O.
CASTILLEJA COCCINEA   SCROPHULARIACEAE
Tea to destroy your enemies.

indian physic, bowman's root, gillenia, american ipecac, american ipecacuanha   M.
GILLENIA STIPULATA   ROSACEAE
G. TRIFOLIATA
CAUTION SUICIDAL: IN LARGE DOSES PRODUCES VERTIGO, HEAT AND
GREAT PROSTRATION OF STRENGTH. Mild tea is emetic; slight doses good for
asthma; colds; with culver's root and boneset leaves for inactive liver; tincture of
root for milksick; poultice for leg swelling; roots for rheumatism; cold root tea or
chewed root for bee and other stings; for toothache; tea for kidneys.

indian pink, un-s-te-tla   M.
SPIGELIA MARILANDICA   LOGANIACEAE
Tea for worms.

indian pipe, fit root, ice plant   M.
MONOTROPA UNIFLORA   ERICACEAE
Root pulverized and given children for fits; for epilepsy and convulsions; juice and
water to wash sore eyes; rub crushed plant on bunions or warts.

indian poke, american white hellebore, false hellebore   M.
VERATRUM VIRIDE   LILIACEAE
Ingredient in liniment for pains or sore muscles.

indian tobacco, lobelia   M, O.
LOBELIA INFLATA   CAMPANULACEAE
Strong emetic; for croup; asthma and phthisic; tincture in small doses prevents
colics and croup; used for bites and stings; root poultice for boils and body aches; rub
leaves on sores, aches, stiff neck, chapped places; chew for sore throat; use to smoke
out gnats; smoke to break tobacco habit.

indigo — blue false, blue wild, wild   M, D.
BAPTISIA AUSTRALIS   FABACEAE
B. TINCTORIA
Hold hot tea on tooth for toothache; emetic; purgative; poultice to allay inflammation
and stop mortification; hold root tea or beaten root against tooth for toothache; cold
tea will stop vomiting; blue dye.

ipecac, ipecacuanha   M.
CEPHAELIS IPECACUANHA   Intro.   RUBIACEAE
Emetic; one teaspoon powdered root to six tablespoons warm water, take spoonful
every few minutes until it works; diaphoretic; expectorant; and stops violent
hemorrhaging from lungs and womb when given in small doses.

iris — crested dwarf, dwarf; blue flag   M.
IRIS CRISTATA   IRIDACEAE
I. VERNA
I. VIRGINICA
Drink tea for liver; root is ingredient in decoction for yellowish urine; stew pulverized
root in hogs' lard, sheep suet, and beeswax to make salve for ulcers.

ironweed — purple, yellow   M.
VERONIA GLAUCA   ASTERACEAE
V. NOVEBORACENSIS
Tea for blood; tea for monthly period; root tea to relieve afterbirth pains; steep
bruised roots of this and sneeze weed, give to women immediately after childbirth,
will prevent menstruation for two years; root tea held in mouth for loose teeth; root
tea for stomach ulcers or hemmorhage.

ivy, poison; poison oak   M.
RHUS RADICANS   ANACARDIACEAE
R. TOXICODENDRON
Decoction as emetic.

jack-in-the-pulpit, indian turnip   M.
ARISAEMA TRIPHYLLUM   ARACEAE
Stimulant; expectorant; diaphoretic; carminative; colds; dry coughs; consumptions; ointment of green twigs stewed in hogs lard for scald head; ringworm,
tetterworm and scrofulous sores; root poultice for headaches; beat up boiled roots
with meal to poutice boils; drink tea for irritations of throat; liniment.

jerusalem oak, mexican tea, vermifuge   M.
CHENOPODIUM BOTRYS   Intro.   CHENOPODIACEAE
Boil any part of plant in sweet milk for worms; boil seeds and sugar for worms; warm
root tea drunk in winter for fever diseases; drink and moisten head with cold tea for
colds and headache.

jewelweed — orange, yellow; spotted touch-me-not   M.
IMPATIENS CAPENSIS   BALSAMINACEAE
I. PALLIDA
Stems are part of decoction, for easy delivery, with yellow pine cones, speedwell root,
and red elm bark; bathe private parts in warm decoction to speed up delivery;
ingredient in green corn medicine; rub crushed leaves on child's sour stomach; leaf
tea for measles; root tea for "bold hives" in babies; rub juice of seven blossoms on
ivy poisoning.

jimson weed   M.
DATURA STRAMONIUM   Intro.   SOLANACEAE
Smoke for asthma; wilt leaves to poultice boils.

job's tears, mother of corn, se-lu-oo-tsi   M.
COIX LACRYMA-JOBI   Intro.   POACEAE
Seed for beads;seeds for bread occasionally; seeds strung around baby's neck for
teething; long strands for other medicinal purposes.

joe-pye weed, queen of the meadow, blowgun weed, gravel root, trumpet weed, water
dipper   M.
EUPATORIUM MACULATUM   ASTERACEAE
E. PURPUREM
Root is diuretic; for gout; dropsy; rheumatism; female problems; roots used in

decoction with another plant for difficult urination; section of stem used to blow or spray medicine; bathe in root infusion of this after becoming sick from odor of corpse; root tea for building up women during pregnancy; stem used as straw in sucking water from low springs; tea for kidney trouble.

jumpseed   M.
TOVARA VIRGINIANA   POLYGONACEAE
Hot tea of leaves with bark of honey locust for whooping cough.

ladies' tresses   M.
SPIRANTHES LUCIDA   ORCHIDACEAE
Wash infant in warm steep to insure fast, healthy growth; roots with twayblade for urinary trouble.

lady's slipper — pink, yellow; moccasin flower, partridge moccasin   M.
CYPRIPEDIUM ACAULE   ORCHIDACEAE
C. CALCEOLUS
Gather roots in fall or spring for nerves, spasms, fits, hysterical affections; relieves pain; drink tea for diabetes; tea of this and black snakeroot (ARISTOLOCHIA SP.) for stomach cramps; steep roots with bastard toadflax for kidney trouble; tea for rupture pains of men or women; female trouble; root tea for worms; root tea with common chickweed for worms; root tea for colds; stomach ache; hot root tea for flu; neuralgia.

lamb's quarters   -F.
CHENOPODIUM ALBUM   CHENOPODIACEAE
Cooked salad greens to keep healthy.

larkspur, rocket   M, O.
DELPHINIUM AJACIS   Intro.   RANUNCULACEAE
D. TRICORNE
Tea for heart; root makes cows drunk and kills them.

laurel, mountain; calico bush; spoonwood   M, O.
KALMIA LATIFOLIA   ERICACEAE
Ingredient in liniment; rub bristly edges of ten to twelve leaves over skin for rheumatism; leaf ooze rubbed into scratched skin of ball players to prevent cramps; leaf salve for healing; crush leaves to rub brier scratches; wash with tea to get rid of pests; carving.

leafcup, bear's foot   M.
POLYMNIA UVEDALIA   ASTERACEAE
Poultice of root to allay inflammations; bruised root for burns; salve for cuts and burns; for rheumatism; for white swelling; bruised root in hog's lard for itch; ingredient in decoction for expelling afterbirth.

leek, house; hen and chickens   M.
SEMPERVIVUM TECTORUM   Intro.   CRASSULACEAE
Wilt, place on corns to remove them; squeeze out juice and warm for earache.

lettuce — field, shawnee, wild   M, F.
LACTUCA CANADENSIS   ASTERACEAE
Drink tea for milksick; stimulant; relieves pain; produces sleep; ingredient in a green corn medicine; tea for calming nerves; cooked greens.

lily, trout; dog's tooth violet, mountain trout   M, O.
ERYTHRONIUM AMERICANUM   LILIACEAE
Root tea will break fever; crush warmed leaves and pour juice over wound that won't heal; ingredient in infusion for fainting; chew root and spit into river to make fish bite.

lily — turk's cap, wild yellow   M, F.
LILIUM CANADENSE   LILIACEAE
Decoction of boiled tubers to make child fleshy and fat; root infusion for flux; variety of uses for rheumatism; root flour for bread eaten in famine times.

liquorice   M.
GLYCYRRHIZA GLABRA   Intro.   FABACEAE
For coughs; asthma; hoarseness; an expectorant.

liquorice, white wild   M.
GALIUM CIRCAEZANS   RUBIACEAE
For asthma; coughs; hoarseness; an expectorant.

lizardtail   M.
SAURURUS CERNUUS   SAURURACEAE
Roots roasted and mashed for poultice.

lobelia, pale spike   M.
LOBELIA SPICATA   CAMPANULACEAE
Ingredient in medicine for arm shakes and trembles.

locust — black, purple, yellow   M, O.
ROBINIA PSEUDO-ACACIA   FABACEAE
R. HISPIDA
Chew bark of root as an emetic; hold beat up root on tooth for toothache; fence posts; bows; pegs for log cabins; sills for house; tea for cow tonic; blowgun darts.

locust, honey   M, F, O.
GLEDITSIA TRIACANTHOS   FABACEAE
Pods to sweeten worm medicine; ingredient in drink for dyspepsia from overeating; **bark tea of this and hawthorn is drunk or bathed in by ball players to ward off tacklers; bark tea, with or without the leaves of virginia knotweed, for whooping cough; pod tea for measles; pulp of seed makes pleasing drink; fence posts.**

loosestrife   M.
LYTHRUM LANCEOLATUM   LYTHRACEAE
Tea for kidneys.

loosestrife — four-leaf, whorled   M.
LYSIMACHIA QUADRIFOLIA   PRIMULACEAE
For kidney problems; tea for female trouble; root decoction for bowel trouble.

lousewort, common; wood betony   M.
PEDICULARIS CANADENSIS   SCROPHULARIACEAE
For bloody discharge from bowels; root steep rubbed on sores; ingredient in cough medicine; hot root decoction for stomach ache; put in dog bed to de-louse pups; infusion drunk for flux; to rid sheep of lice.

lupine   M.
LUPINUS PERENNIS   FABACEAE

Drink and wash with cold tea to check hemorrhage and vomiting; soak head in tea to stop vomiting.

madder, field   -D.
SHERADIA ARVENSIS   Intro.   RUBIACEAE
Red or rose dye.

magnolia — bigleaf, great leaved; cucumber tree, big leaves   M, O.
MAGNOLIA MACROPHYLLA   MAGNOLIACEAE
M. ACUMINATA
One of six ingredients in steam bath for indigestion or biliousness with swelling abdomen and yellowish skin; hold warm bark decoction of this and hophornbeam in mouth for toothache; bark tea for stomach ache or cramps; bark is ingredient in medicine for bloody flux; snuff hot tea of bark for sinus; furniture; pulpwood; lumber.

mallow, round-leaved; cheeses   M.
MALVA NEGLECTA   Intro.   MALVACEAE
Put flowers in oil, mix with tallow to use on sores.

maple — green, striped, white; moosewood   -O.
ACER PENSYLVANICUM   ACERACEAE
Firewood.

maple — hard, sugar   -F, O.
ACER SACCHARUM   ACERACEAE
Sugar from juice; furniture; lumber; carving.

maple — red, silver, soft   M,O.
ACER RUBRUM   ACERACEAE
A. SACCHARINUM
Inner bark boiled to syrup, made into pills, dissolve them in water and use as wash for sore eyes; tea for dysentery; drink tea for hives; steep bark with those of white oak, black oak and chestnut for female trouble; bark tea for cramps; hot bark tea for measles; lumber; carving; furniture; baskets.

marigold   M, D.
TAGETES ERECTA   Intro.   ASTERACEAE
Bathe in tea for exzema; **flower for yellow dye.**

mayapple, mandrake   M, F, O.
PODOPHYLLUM PELTATUM   BERBERIDACEAE
JOINTS OF ROOTS ARE POISON. USE ONLY THOSE PORTIONS BETWEEN THE JOINTS. Root antihelminthic; boiled root — purgative; drop of juice of fresh root in ear for deafness; powdered root on ulces and sores; gather root in late fall, dry in shade, soak corn in root ooze before planting to keep off crows and insects; root soaked in whiskey drunk for rheumatism; eat to correct constipation; fruit for food.

milkweed — common, four leaved; silkweed   M, O.
ASCLEPIAS PERENNIS   ASCLEPIADACEAE
A. SYRIACA   Intro.
A. QUADRIFOLIA
Drink root tea with root of virgin's bower for backache; root tea for venereal diseases; laxative; for gravel; dropsy; rub on warts to remove them; tea for milksick (mastitis); fiber of plant for bowstrings.

milkweed, ground; eyebane, flowering spurge M.
EUPHORBIA MACULATA EUPHORBIACEAE
E. COROLLATA
Tea to stop bleeding after childbirth; root for toothache; bruised root infusion for urinary diseases; juice rubbed on skin eruptions, especially on children's heads; purgative; decoction drunk for gonorrhea and similar diseases; juice is ointment for sores and sore nipples; decoction with herbs for cancer.

milkwort M.
POLYGALA VERTICILLATA POLYGALACEAE
Tea for summer complaint.

mint, downy wood M.
BLEPHILIA CILIATA LAMIACEAE
Poultice of leaves for headache.

mint — mealy, mountain M, F.
PYCNANTHEMUM FLEXUOSUM LAMINACEAE
P. INCANUM
Leaf poultice for headache; tea for fevers and colds; tea of leaves for heart trouble; bathe inflamed penis with warm tea; tea for upset stomach; drink tea with green corn to avoid diarrhea; food.

mint, wild M., F.
MENTHA ARVENIS LAMINACEAE
Tea for fever; food.

mistletoe M.
PHORADENDRON SEROTINUM LORANTHACEAE
Dried and pulverized is good for epilepsy or fits, best if from oak; steeped in hot water is medicine for pregnant women; bathe head in tea ooze for headache; to cure lovesickness, vomit for four days, then drink mistletoe tea; tea for high blood pressure.

mother-wort M.
LEONURUS CARDIACA Intro. LAMIACEAE
Stimulant; for nervous and hysterical affections; fainting and disease of the stomach.

mud-plantain, swamp lily M.
HETERANTHERA RENIFORMIS Intro. PONTEDERIACEAE
Hot root poultice for inflamed wounds and sores.

mulberry — red, white M, F.
MORUS RUBRA MARACEAE
M. ALBA Intro.
Drink bark tea to check dysentery; purgative; worms; laxative; food.

mullein, common; mule tail M.
VERBASCUM THAPSUS Intro. SCROPHULARIACEAE
Ingredient in drink for pains; rub leaves under armpits for prickly rash; mix leaf decoction of this and chestnut with brown sugar or honey for cough syrup; root tea for kidneys; bathe legs in root infusion for dropsy; root or leaf tea for female trouble; wrap leaves around neck for mumps; put flowers in bottle of oil, use on sores; scald leaves and use on swollen glands.

mushroom, beefsteak -F.
FISTULINA HEPATICA BOLETACEAE
Cooked food.

mushroom, devil's snuffbox, puffball M.
LYCOPERDON PERLATUM LYCOPERDALES
L. PYRIFORME
Break open when dry, put snuff on sores.

mustard — black, field, white M.
BRASSICA NIGRA Intro. BRASSICACEAE
B. NAPUS Intro.
B. HIRTA Intro.
Increases appetite; stimulant; tonic; for fever and ague; nervous fever; dropsy; palsy; phthisic or asthma; poultice for croup.

mustard, hedge M, F.
SISYMBRIUM OFFICINALE Intro. BRASSICACEAE
Poultice for croup; cooked salad greens.

nettle — bear, stinging M,O.
URTICA DIOICA Intro. URTICACEAE
Medicine for upset stomach; tea for ague; twisted stems for bow strings.

nettle — bull, horse M.
SOLANUM CAROLINENSE SOLANACEAE
For ulcers and proud flesh; cut up berries and fry in grease, use grease to cure mange in dogs; wilt to use on poison ivy; put crushed leaves in sweet milk to kill flies; leaf tea for worms; root beads around baby's neck when teething; gargle seed tea for sore throat; seed tea for goiter.

new jersey tea, red root M.
CEANOTHUS AMERICANUS RHAMNACEAE
Hold root tea on aching tooth; hot root tea for bowel complaint.

oak — black, post, red, shingle, spanish, white M, O.
QUERCUS VELUTINA FAGACEAE
Q. STELLATA
Q. RUBRA
Q. IMBRICARIA
Q. FALCATA
Q. ALBA
Bark is astringent; tonic; antiseptic; after long intermittent fevers; indigestion; chronic dysentery or any debility of the system; bathe in it for chills and fevers; bark is emetic; bark tea applied to sore, chapped skin; chew bark for mouth sores; bark tea of black oak, red maple and chestnut for female trouble; drink for milky urine; bark tea for relief of asthma; decoction of inner bark for lost voice; splits for baskets; lumber; firewood; furniture; woven chair bottoms; railroad ties; wagon spokes and rims; corn beater or mortar (Ka-no-na); leaves of this and other large-leaved species are used to wrap dough for bread making.

oak, chestnut -O.
QUERCUS PRINUS FAGACEAE
Bark for tan bark; railroad ties.

oak, pin
QUERCUS PALUSTRIS   FAGACEAE
Pins or small pegs.

old field apricot, maypop, passion flower   M, F.
PASSIFLORA INCARNATA   PASSIFLORACEAE
Pound root and apply to brier or locust wounds to draw out inflammation; ingredient
in root tea for boils; beat up root in warm water, drop into ear for earache; root tea
for babies who are hard to wean, give to six month old, it will drop off the breast at one
year; tea for liver; a social drink; fruit is edible.

onion — nodding, wild   M, F.
ALLIUM CERNUUM   LILIACEAE
Drink tea for colic; fry and put on chest for croup; juice for hives and croup in
children; colds; sore throat; phthisic; liver complaints; after horsemint tea for
gravel and dropsy; poultice feet in nervous fever; food.

orchid, yellow-fringed   M, O.
HABENARIA CILIARIS   ORCHIDACEAE
Cold root infusion for headache; drink warm tea every hour for flux; piece of root on
hook to make fish bite.

panic grass   -O.
PANICUM SP.   POACEAE
Stems are used for padding inside of moccasins.

parsley   M.
PETROSELINUM CRISPUM   Intro.   APIACEAE
Top and root tea for kidneys and bladder; dropsy; female obstructions; lying-in
women whose discharges are too scant; abortive.

parsnip, wild   M.
PASTINACA SATIVA   Intro.   APIACEAE
For sharp pains.

partridge berry, hive vine, squaw vine, winter clover   M, F.
MITCHELLA REPENS   RUBIACEAE
Diaphoretic; diuretic; boil in new milk for dysentery and piles; to facilitate
childbirth; root tea with rattlesnake weed for bowel complaint; for baby before it
takes the breast; for monthly period pains; for pregnant cat; for her kittens; tea for
hives; for sore nipples; food.

pawpaw   -F, O.
ASIMINA TRILOBA   ANNONACEAE
Food; inner bark for strong ropes and string.

pea, butterfly   M.
CLITORIA MARIANA   FABACEAE
For sore mouth (thrush) hold tea in mouth for ten to twenty minutes and repeat
several times.

peach   M, F.
PRUNUS PERSICA   Intro.   ROSACEAE
Tea of any part as purgative; strong tea for fever; decoction for worms; skin
diseases; bark steep for cough medicine; apply cold bark tea and soda to piles; wring
leaves in cold water to bathe swelling; pour cold water over scraped bark, drink to

stop vomiting; tea of leaves for sick stomach; teaspoon of parched seed kernels for worms; fruit for food.

pearly everlasting M.
ANAPHALIS MARGARITACEA Intro. ASTERACEAE
Dried leaves smoked for catarrh; warm tea for cold; smoke or chew leaves for colds; for throat infection; leaves and stems smoked for bronchial cough; dried leaves substitute for chewing tobacco; make cold tea pour,over hot rock and breathe fumes to cure headache or blindness caused by sun's radiance.

pears -F.
PYRUS COMMUNIS Intro. ROSACEAE
Fruit for food.

peas -F.
PISUM SATIVUM FABACEAE
Food.

pennyroyal M, O.
HEDEOMA PULEGOIDES LAMIACEAE
Decoction is stimulant; diaphoretic; expectorant; for colds, coughs and whooping cough; tea for obstructed menses; fever; hold beaten leaves in mouth for toothache; tea for flux; leaf poultice for headaches; rub leaves on for insect repellent.

pennyworth M.
OBOLARIA VIRGINICA GENTIANACEAE
Diaphoretic; for colds; coughs; colic.

pepper and salt, harbinger of spring M.
ERIGENIA BULBOSA APIACEAE
Chew for toothache.

pepper, black M, F.
PIPER NIGRUM Intro. PIPERACEAE
Stimulus and slightly astringent; to season food.

pepper, bush; mountain sweet M.
BERBERIS CANADENSIS BERBERIDACEAE
Scrape bark to make tea for loose bowels.

pepper — cayenne, red M.
CAPSICUM FRUTESCENS Intro. SOLANACEAE
Powerful stimulant; colds; colics; poultice applied to soles of feet in nervous or low fevers; poultice gangrene.

peppergrass, chicken pepper M, F, O.
LEPIDIUM VIRGINICUM Intro. BRASSICACEAE
Apply bruised root to skin to draw blister quickly; poultice for croup; food; mix with chicken feed to make them lay; tea for sick chickens.

peppermint, spearmint M, F.
MENTHA PIPERITA Intro. LAMIACEAE
M. SPICATA Intro.
Stimulant; to check vomiting; relieve hysterics; for affections of stomach and bowels; dispels flatulence and remove colic pains; relieve cramps; smell and wet temples to remove nervous headache; for cholera infantum; remedy for suppression

of urine and gravelly affection; tincture applied externally to piles; tea for upset stomach; tea to depress fevers; for colds; for foods; used to flavor foods and medicine.

persimmon, common   M, F.
DIOSPYROS VIRGINIANA   EBENACEAE
Astringent; for venereal diseases; sore throat and mouth; syrup for thrush; wash for piles; one of six ingredients in steam bath for indigestion or biliousness with swelling of abdomen and yellowish skin; boil down for bloody discharge from bowels; chew bark for heartburn; make bark infusion of persimmon, alder, white walnut and wild cherry for toothache; pour cold water over bark, drink for bile; tea for liver; fruit for food.

peruvian bark   M.
CINCHONA LEDGERIANA   Intro.   RUBIACEAE
Tonic; drink tea for impotence.

phacelia, common   M.
PHACELIA PURSHII   HYDROPHYLLACEAE
Pack swollen joints with plant.

phacelia, small flowered; oo-s-te-s-gi   -F.
PHACELIA DUBIA   HYDROPHYLLACEAE
Cooked greens for food.

pine — black, jack, scrub, spruce, virginia   M, O.
PINUS VIRGINIANA   PINACEAE
P. GLABRA
Syrup for pregnant women with cough; for catarrh (ulcer of the lungs); chronic rheumatism; venereal disease; applied externally for swelled testicles caused by mumps; externally for swelling of the breasts; oil for colds and bathing painful joints; needles, with bark of witch hazel and spicewood in hot tea to break out fever; needles with summer grape stem and apple juice drunk by ball players for wind; needle steam to relieve cold; root tea with small rose and alder for piles; boil root, skim off turpentine, spread on deer's skin for drawing plaster; stimulant; gentle laxative; tea from bud or inside bark for hard dry coughs; for worms; hysterics; colics; gout; weak back or kidneys; child-bed-fevers; tar for consumption; tar plaster externally for scaldhead; tetterworm; stone bruise and foul sores or ulcers; tea of boughs for colds; to break out measles; powder resin to sprinkle on sores; chew bark to check bowels; needles used in basketry; pine branches are burned in cooking vessels and the ashes are thrown on the rekindled hearth fire after a death in the home; needles or gum to scent soap.

pine — loblolly, pitch, shortleaf, table mountain, white, yellow   -O.
PINUS TAEDA   PINACEAE
P. RIGIDA
P. ECHINATA
P. PUNGENS
P. STROBUS
Lumber; carving; canoes thirty to forty feet long.

pineapple weed   M.
MATRICARIA MATRICARIOIDES   Intro.   ASTERACEAE
Tea to keep regular.

plantain — black, bracted, broad-leaf, english, green M, F.
PLANTAGO ARISTATA Intro. PLANTAGINACEAE
P. LANCEOLATA Intro.
P. MAJOR Intro.
Wilt or scald leaf for burns, bruises or beat for poultice; dressing for blisters, ulcers, or sores; leaf infusion with rush will strengthen a child learning to crawl or walk; root tea for dysentery; leaf poultice for headache; apply wilted leaves to yellowjacket sting; tea to bathe swelling; tea to check discharge; tea to check babies' bowels; use tea as douche; tea for poisonous bites, stings and snakebites; for bowel complaints; bloody urine; juice for sore eyes; green plantain (PLANTAGO MAJOR) as cooked greens.

plantain lily, narrow leaf M.
HOSTA JAPONICA Intro. LILIACEAE
Rub leaf tea on swollen parts of legs and feet, caused by almost invisible insects, after scratching; warm root tea for coughing, spitting blood.

plantain, rattlesnake M.
GOODYERA PUBESCENS ORCHIDACEAE
G. REPENS
Hold tea in mouth for toothache; cold leaf tea for colds; kidneys; and with whiskey will improve the appetite; drip ooze into sore eyes; decoction of this alder, wild cherry, wild ginger and yellowroot is a good blood tonic and builds appetite; emetic; wilt leaves to draw out burn.

plantain, white M.
ANTENNARIA PLANTAGINIFOLIA ASTERACEAE
For bowel complaint (especially children) use tea of entire plant; tea for excessive discharge in monthly period.

plum, wild; sloe M, F.
PRUNUS AMERICANA ROSACEAE
Bark tea for kidneys and bladder; use bark to make cough syrup; fruit for food, juice and jelly.

pokeweed, pokeberry M, F, O.
PHYTOLACCA AMERICANA PHYTOLACCACEAE
Roots and berries for rheumatism; poultice for nervous fevers, ulcers, swellings; with other ingredients for white-swelling; salve for cancers and ulcerous sores; **sprinkle dried, crushed roots on old sores; root tea for eczema; cold tea of powdered** root for kidneys; berry wine to relieve rheumatism; root tea for blood; berry tea for arthritis; cooked greens are good for building the blood; crushed berries add color to canned fruit.

poplar — tulip, yellow; tsi-yu, tulip tree M, F, O.
LIRIODENDRON TULIPIFERA MAGNOLIACEAE
Bark of root in tea for fever; poultices; bark for dyspepsy, dysentery and rheumatism; for cholera infantum; for women with hysterics and weakness; decoction to bathe snakebite; one of six ingredients in steambath for indigestion or biliousness with swelling of abdomen and yellowish skin; blow decoction on fractured limb, wounds, boils; bark tea for pinworms; bark for cough syrup; honey; for canoes, thirty to forty feet long; lumber, pulpwood; cradles.

poppy, white M.
PAPAVER SOMNIFERUM Intro. PAPAVERACEAE

Stimulant is small doses; larger dose produces sleep and relieves pain; soothes and tranquilizes system; antispasmodic; removes cramps.

potato, sweet   -F.
IMPOMOEA BATATAS   Intro.   CONVOLVULACEAE
Food.

potato, white; nightshade   M, F.
SOLANUM TUBEROSUM   SOLANACEAE
S. NIGRUM
Tea of leaves and stem if lonesome because of death in family; emetic; young leaves of S. NIGRUM as potherb; root of S. TUBEROSUM as food.

potato, wild; cowbane   -F.
OXYPOLIS RIGIDIOR   CONVOLVULACEAE
Root is baked and eaten.

potato vine, wild; trumpet vine   M, F, O.
IPOMOEA PANDURATA   CONVOLVULACEAE
Diuretic; for gravel; dropsy; suppression of urine; laxative; expectorant; for coughs; asthma; consumption; root tea for cholera morbis (bowel complaint); root poultice for rheumatism; food from root; soak sweet potatoes in vine tea before planting to keep away bugs and moles.

prickly ash   M.
ZANTHOXYLUM AMERICANA   RUTACEAE
Tea to bathe swollen joints.

pumpkin, pumpion   M, F.
CUCURBITA PEPO   CUCURBITACEAE
Diuretic; for gravel; dropsy; gives immediate relief of scalding of the urine and spasms of the urinary passage; an ingredient in green corn medicine; eat browned seeds to stop bedwetting; eat seeds for worms; food.

purslane, common; chickweed   M.
PORTULACA OLERACEA   Intro.   PORTULACACEAE
Ingredient in decoction for worms; juice for earache.

puttyroot, adam and eve   M,O.
APLECTRUM HYEMALE   ORCHIDACEAE
To make children fleshy and fat; to endow children with the gift of eloquence; root are put in the slop to make hogs fat.

queen anne's lace   M.
DAUCUS CAROTA   Intro.   APIACEAE
Bathe with tea for swelling.

queen's delight   M.
STILLINGIA SYLVATICA   EUPHORBIACEAE
Root decoction or tincture for venereal or clap in worst forms.

rabbit tobacco, life everlasting   M.
GNAPHALIUM OBTUSIFOLIUM   ASTERACEAE
Decoction for colds; use with carolina vetch for rheumatism; sweat bath for various diseases; warm liquid is blown down throat through joe-pye-weed stem for clogged throat (diptheria); ingredient in medicine for local pains, muscular cramps, and

twitching; chew for sore mouth or throat; smoke for asthma; cough syrup.

ragweed — common, great
AMBROSIA ARTEMISIIFOLIA
A. TRIFIDA
M.
ASTERACEAE

Ingredient in green corn medicine; crush leaves and rub on poison insect sting; tea for pneumonia; leaf tea drunk for fever; rubbed on for hives; for infected toes apply the juice squeezed from wilted leaves.

ragwort, golden; squaw weed
SENECIO AUREUS
M.
ASTERACEAE

Tea for heart trouble; tea to prevent pregnancy.

ramps
ALLIUM TRICOCCUM
M, F.
LILIACEAE

Warm juice for earache; eat for croup; colds; spring tonic; for food.

raspberry — bear, black, purple-flowering, wild red; thimbleberry shrub,
yun-oo-gi-s-ti
RUBUS ODORATUS
R. OCCIDENTALIS
R. IDAEUS   Intro.
M, F.
ROSACEAE

Chew root for cough; leaves highly astringent; decoction for bowel complaint; wash for old and foul sores or ulcers; strong tea of red raspberry leaves for pains at childbirth; scratch rheumatism with thorny branch; ingredient in decoction for menstrual period; acts as emetic and purgative; tea drunk as tonic for boils; roots for toothache; fruit for food.

redbud
CERCIS CANADENSIS
M, F.
FABACEAE

Bark tea for whooping cough; children eat the blossoms.

red-root
LACHNANTHES CAROLINIANA
M.
HAEMODORACEAE

Root — astringent; strong decoction wash for cancer; for bowel complaints; spitting blood; flooding; bloody piles; sore mouth and throat; ingredient in decoction for venereal disease.

rhododendron, great
RHODODENDRON MAXIMUM
M, O.
ERICACEAE

Ingredient in liniment for pains; leaf decoction with mountain laurel and doghobble for rheumatism, throw clumps of leaves into a fire and dance around it to bring cold weather; tea of leaves for heart trouble; bind leaves on forehead for headaches; carving; spoons; pipes.

rhubarb
RHEUM RHAPONTICUM   Intro.
M, F.
POLYGONACEAE

Mild purgative; astringent; strengthening; dysentery; tea for constipation; food.
LEAVES POISONOUS.

rich weed, horse balm, stone root
COLLINSONIA CANADENSIS
M, O.
LAMIACEAE

Ingredient in cure for swollen breasts; mash flowers and leaves, use as a deodorant; tea to drench horses with colic.

rich weed, toe itch
M.

PILEA PUMILA   URTICACEAE
Infusion to reduce excessive hunger of children; rub stems between the toes for itching.

rose-pink, field pink   M.
SABATIA ANGULARIS   GENTIANACEAE
Tea for periodic pains.

rose, wild   M.
ROSA PALUSTRIS   ROSACEAE
Boil roots, drink for dysentery; bark and root tea for worms.

rosin weed   M.
SILPHIUM COMPOSITUM   ASTERACEAE
Strong stimulant for whites; for weakly females.

rue anemone, early meadow rue   M.
THALICTRUM THALICTROIDES   RANUNCULACEAE
T. DIOICUM
Root tea for diarrhea and vomiting.

rue, common garden   M.
RUTA GRAVEOLENS   Intro.   RUTACEAE
Top or leaves boiled to syrup for worms; for hysterics add to whiskey; for palsy; poultice for gangrenous parts.

rush, common; wiregrass   M, O.
JUNCUS EFFUSUS   JUNCACEAE
J. TENUIS
Decoction to dislodge spoiled salvia; wash babies in tea for strength; tea with plantain to prevent infant lameness; string to bind up dough in oak leaves for cooking bread.

saffron   M.
CROCUS SATIVUS   Intro.   IRIDACEAE
Good for children's hives; jaundice; red gum; eruptive diseases.

sage — blue, garden   M.
SALVIA LYRATA   LAMIACEAE
S. OFFICINALIS   Intro.
Tea for laxative; tea for colds; coughs; nervous debility; weakly females; phlegmatic habits; syrup of leaves and honey for asthma; mild diaphoretic; tea to check bowels.

saint andrew's cross, saint peter's wort, saint john's wort, piney weed   M.
HYPERICUM HYPERICOIDES   HYPERICACEAE
H. PERFORATUM
H. GENTIANOIDES
Chew root, swallow portion and apply rest to snakebite; bathe infants in root tea for strength; drink tea for fever; crush plant and sniff for nosebleed; tea for bloody flux; bowel complaint; decoction of mad dog's skullcap, hairy skullcap and squaw vine drunk to promote menstruation; rub milky substance on sores; for venereal disease.

sarsaparilla, wild   M.
ARALIA NUDICAULIS   ARALIACEAE
Root tea for blood tonic.

sarsaparilla, yellow M.
MENISPERMUM CANADENSE MENISPERMACEAE
Root for diseases of the skin; laxative; weakly females; weak stomachs and bowels; for venereal diseases.

sassafras M, F, O.
SASSAFRAS ALBIDUM LAURACEAE
Tea to purify blood; skin diseases; rheumatism; venereal; ague; poultice wounds and sores; wash for sore eyes; plant is ingredient in medicine for worms; root bark steep for diarrhea or flux; colds; bark tea for overfatness; beverage tea of roots and barks; used to scent soap; furniture; mix flowers with beans for planting.

savory, summer M.
SATUREJA HORTENSIS Intro. LAMIACEAE
Sniff of leaves for headache.

sedge M.
CAREX SP. CYPERACEAE
Leaf tea to check bowels.

selfheal, ga-ni-qui-li-s-ki , heal-all M, F, O.
PRUNELLA VULGARIS LAMIACEAE
Bathe bruises in root tea; cold infusion to bathe burns; bathe in tea to control diabetic sores; tea to heal cuts; tea to bathe pimply face; eat for cooked greens; used to flavor other medicines.

senna — american, wild M.
CASSIA MARILANDICA FABACEAE
C. HEBECARPA
Root poultice for sores; tea for fever and disease called "blacks" (hands and eye sockets turn black);cathartic; purgative — good for children; hot root steep for heart trouble; tea with partridge plant for fainting spells; ingredient in medicine for pneumonia; root tea for children's fever; tea for cramps.

sensitive plant, wild; partridge pea M.
CASSIA NICTITANS FABACEAE
C. FASCICULATA
Root medicine to keep ball players from tiring; tea with wild senna for fainting spells.

serviceberry tree, sarvis, shadbush M, F.
AMELANCHIER ARBOREA ROSACEAE
One ingredient in tea for worms; ingredient in tea for diarrhea; tea for spring tonic; berries for food.

seven bark, wild hydrangea M.
HYDRANGEA ARBORESCENS SAXIFRAGACEAE
Inner bark and leaves stimulant; antiseptic; anti-emetic; good for ulcers; tumors; sprains; ingredient in tea for menstrual period; purgative; bark infusion to induce vomiting to throw off disordered bile; make cold tea of green inner bark to stop vomiting in children; bind on scarped bark for burns and risings; poultice for sore or swollen muscles; chew bark for stomach trouble; for high blood pressure.

shepherd's purse -F.
CAPSELLA BURSA-PASTORIS Intro. BRASSICACEAE
Cooked greens.

shin leaf M.
PYROLA ELLIPTICA ERICACEAE
P. ROTUNDIFOLIA
Stick on cuts and sores to heal them.

silverbells -O.
HALESIA CAROLINA STYRACACEAE
Lumber.

skullcap — blue, hairy, mad dog; ga-ni-qui-li-s-ki M.
SCUTELLARIA LATERIFLORA LAMIACEAE
S. ELLIPTICA
S. INCANA
Root is ingredient in a kidney medicine; decoction for nerves; root tea for monthly
period; for diarrhea; ingredient in medicine for breast pains; ingredient in medicine
for expelling afterbirth.

smartweed, knotweed M, O.
POLYGONUM HYDROPIPER POLYGONACEAE
P. AVICULARE Intro.
For gravel and painful urination; poultice for swelled and inflamed parts; bloody
urine; scald head; root infusion to halt flux in children; mix tea with meal to poultice
pain; rub leaves on children's thumb to prevent thumb-sucking; used to poison fish.

snakeroot, black M.
SANICULA SMALLII APIACEAE
Tea with pink lady's slipper for stomach cramps; tea for colic; liniment.

snakeroot, black; doll's eyes, white baneberry, white bugbane M.
ACTAEA PACHYPODA RANUNCULACEAE
Root tea for gargle; to cure itch; tea to relieve and rally a patient at point of death;
WILL KILL TEETH OF YOUNG PEOPLE IF NOT CAREFUL WITH IT.

snakeroot — black, virginia; little-root, long root M.
ARISTOLOCHIA SERPENTARIA ARISTOLOCHIACEAE
Tonic for typhus fevers; ague and fever; diuretic; antiseptic; gargle for sore throat;
stops mortification and prevents putrefaction in the bowels; for persons of weak,
phlegmatic habits; drink for relief of sharp pains in the breast; wash for headache;
for dizziness or fainting; "black-yellow" diseases; drink tea or chew root for colds;
drink cold infusion of entire plant to relieve pain and prevent fainting; tea for
rheumatism; obstructions; anodyne; for pleurisy and sharp darting pains; drink for
coughs; chew root and spit on snakebite; bruise root and hold on tooth for toothache;
hold against nose made sore by constant blowing; stimulant; tonic; dyspepsia.

snakeroot, sampson M.
PSORALEA PSORALIOIDES FABACEAE
Tonic; for obstructed menstruation; colic and indigestion; diaphoretic; drink tea to
check discharge.

snakeroot, seneka; milk-weed, milkwort M.
POLYGALA SENEGA POLYGALACEAE
For snakebites, chew root, swallow sufficient quantity and apply the rest to the
wound, repeat as necessary; sudorific; diuretic; emmenagogue; cathartic; for colds;
pleurisy; rheumatism; inflammatory complaints; dropsy; swellings; croup; root tea
or powder is expectorant and cathartic in large doses.

snakeroot, white   M.
EUPATORIUM RUGOSUM   ASTERACEAE
Root is stimulant; tonic; diuretic; for ague and fever; gravel and diseases of the
urinary organs; tea for diarrhea.

sneezeweed   M.
HELENIUM AUTUMNALE   ASTERACEAE
Use powdered dry leaves to induce sneezing; bruised root steep of this and ironweed
given to woman after childbirth prevents menstruation for two years.

solomon's seal, false   M.
SMILACINA RACEMOSA   LILIACEAE
Bathe sore eyes in cold root steep.

solomon's seal, large; oo-ga-na-s-ta   M,F.
POLYGONATUM BIFLORUM   LILIACEAE
Root is mild tonic for general debility; diseases of the breast or lungs; females
afflicted with whites or profuse menstruation; dysentery; hot bruised root poultice to
draw risings or carbuncles; tea of roasted roots for stomach trouble; roots dried and
beaten used as flour for bread; ground roots can be used as salt; eaten as cooked
greens.

sorrel — purple, yellow wood; sourgrass   M, F.
OXALIS VIOLACEA   OXALIDACEAE
O. CORNICULATA   Intro.
Cold leaf tea will stop vomiting; chew leaves for disordered saliva; mix leaf tea with
sheep grease into salve for sores; children drink and bathe in tea to remove
hookworms; for cancer when it is first started; chew for sore mouth; tea for blood;
chew for sore throat; may be eaten raw.

sorrel — sheep, wild   M, F.
RUMEX ACETOSELLA   Intro.   POLYGONACEAE
Bruise leaves and blossoms, apply as poultice to old sores; may be eaten raw.

sourwood   M, F, O.
OXYDENDRUM ARBOREUM   ERICACEAE
Tonic for dyspepsy; phthisic; asthma; lung diseases; ingredient in tea for diarrhea;
bark ooze for itch; chew for mouth ulcers; tea for nerves; pipestems; arrowshafts;
honey; carving; sled runners; butter paddles; firewood.

speedwell — common, thyme-leaf; purslane   M.
VERONICA OFFICINALIS   Intro.   SCROPHULARIACEAE
V. SERPYLLIAFOLIA   Intro.
Poultice for boils; squeeze out juice and heat for earache; drunk by patient with chills
whenever he feels thirsty; add sugar to tea for cough.

spicewood, allspice tree   M, F.
LINDERA BENZOIN   LAURACEAE
Any part is diaphoretic; colds; coughs; phthisics; croup; for female obstructions;
white swellings; bark steep with dogwood, wild cherry and corn whiskey to break out
measles; boil bark with witch hazel and virginia pine needles for a diaphoretic; tea
for spring tonic; bold hives; blood; cough medicine; beverage; use to flavor possum
or ground hog.

spiderwort, dayflower   M, F.
TRADESCANTIA VIRGINIANA   COMMELINACEAE

Tea with six other ingredients drunk for female ailments or rupture; ingredient in medicine for kidney trouble; tea for stomach ache from overeating; root poultice for cancer; tea for laxative; mash and rub on insect bites.

spignet, spikenard   M.
ARALIA RACEMOSA   ARALIACEAE
Tea of roots and berries is tonic; diaphoretic; antiseptic; astringent; expectorant; for coughs; asthma; diseases of the lungs; for weak backs; fresh wounds and cuts; bathe burns in ooze of beaten roots; bind ooze of root on swelling; for menstrual problems use tea.

spruce, red; he-balsam   M, O.
PICEA RUBENS   PINACEAE
Bough tea for colds; to break out measles; bark used for baskets, lumber.

spanish needles   M.
BIDENS BIPINNATA   Intro.   ASTERACEAE
Chew leaves for sore throat; tea for worms.

squaw vine, pencil flower   M.
STYLOSANTHES BIFLORA   FABACEAE
Hot root tea for female complaint; with other ingredients to promote menstruation.

staggerbush, kill calf, moor-wort   M.
LYONIA MARIANA   ERICACEAE
Tea for toe itch; ground-itch; ulcers.

stargrass, star-root   M.
ALETRIS FARINOSA   LILIACEAE
Tonic for child-bed fever; strengthens stomach and womb; root prevents abortion; for coughs; consumption; diseases of the lungs; rheumatism; strangury; jaundice; flatulent colic.

stargrass, yellow   M.
HYPOXIS HIRSUTA   AMARYLLIDACEAE
Tea for heart.

strawberry, wild   M, F.
FRAGARIA VIRGINIANA   ROSACEAE
For disease of kidneys and bladder; visceral obstructions; jaundice; scurvy; hold fruit in mouth to remove tartar on teeth; tea to calm nerves; tea for dysentery; keep in home to insure happiness; can be eaten raw.

sumac — dwarf, smooth, staghorn   M, F, D.
RHUS COPALLINA   ANACARDIACEAE
R. GLABRA
R. TYPHINA
Pour tea over sunburn blisters; bark tea drunk to make human milk flow abundantly; chew red berries to stop bedwetting; eat to stop vomiting; berries yield black dye shading to red; food.

sumach, white   M.
RHUS VERNIX   ANACARDIACEAE
POISON For clap; asthma; phthisic; ague and fever; gleet or ulcerated bladder; wash for foul ulcers.

sunflower, tall swamp M.
HELIANTHUS GIGANTEUS ASTERACEAE
Sprinkle dry powder to induce sneezing.

sweet fern M.
COMPTONIA PEREGRINA MYRICACEAE
Tea for round worms.

sweetgum M, O.
LIQUIDAMBAR STYRACIFLUA HAMAMELIDACEAE
Gum for drawing plaster; bark tea for nervous patients; rosin or inner bark for diarrhea; flux; dysentery; salve for wounds; sores; ulcers; mix with sheep or cow tallow for itch; bark tea with hearts-a-bustin-with-love, summer grape; sycamore, buckeye, sawbrier and black gum for bad disease; bark tea to stop flooding; hardened gum for chewing gum.

sweet shrub, all spice; bubby root, calycanthus, strawberry shrub M, O.
CALYCANTHUS FLORIDUS CALYCANTHACEAE
Roots are strong emetics; for urinary and bladder complaints; cold bark tea as eyedrops for persons losing eyesight; bark ooze for children's sores; tea for hives; perfume.

sweet william M.
PHLOX MACULATA POLEMONIACEAE
To make children grow and fatten bathe them in a root infusion.

sycamore, big mulberry; buttonwood M, O.
PLATANUS OCCIDENTALIS PLATANACEAE
Roost with carolina hemlock and sawbrier in decoction to aid in expelling afterbirth; for milky urine; dysentery; one of six ingredients in steam bath for indigestion or biliousness with swelling of abdomen and yellowish skin; emetic; purgative; ingredient in decoction for menstrual period; bark tea with sweetgum, heart's-a-bustin-with-love, summer grape, beech, sawbrier and black gum for bad disease; wash infected sore with bark ooze; tea for infant rash; tea of inner bark for measles, cough; buttons; lumber.

tansy M.
TANACETUM VULGARE Intro. ASTERACEAE
Tonic; wear around waist and in shoes to prevent miscarriages and abortions; childs worm medicine; tea for bachache.

tassel flower, pale indian plantain M,F.
CACALIA ATRIPLICIFOLIA ASTERACEAE
Poultice for cuts, bruises and cancer; to draw out blood or poisonous matter use bruised leaf bound over the spot and changed frequently; powdered leaf used as seasoning.

thimbleweed M.
ANEMONE VIRGINICA RANUNCULACEAE
Root tea for whooping cough.

thistle — bull, little, plumed M,O.
CARDUUS LANCEOLATUS Into. ASTERACEAE
C. ALTISSIMUS
Roots as poultice; warm tea of roots for overeating; drink tea of leaves for neuralgia; bruise and boil to poultice sore jaw; down used for tail of blow darts.

thistle, sow   M.
SONCHUS ARVENSIS   Intro.   ASTERACEAE
Tea to calm nerves.

tickseed   M,D.
COREOPSIS TINCTORIA   ASTERACEAE
Root tea for flux; red dye.

tickseed, trefoil; tick trefoil, devil's shoe string   M.
DESMODIUM PERPLEXUM   FABACEAE
D. NUDIFLORUM
Chew roots for sore gums and mouth, including pyorrhea; make tea of roots and bathe body for cramps.

tobacco, wild tobacco   M,O.
NICOTIANA TABACUM   Intro.   SOLANACEAE
N. RUSTICA
Diuretic; emetic; cathartic; antispasmodic; sudorific; expectorant; antihelminthic; dropsy; cramps; locked-jaw; colic; for insect bites apply externally; dizziness and fainting; black-yellow disease; beat up to poultice boils; juice externally for snakebite; blow smoke on toothache; leaf decoction for the great chill, ague; ingredient in medicine for apoplexy; for sharp pains; smoke; used extensively in rituals.

toothwort, crinkled   M,F.
CARDAMINE DIPHYLLA   BRASSICACEAE
Root poultice for headache; chew root for colds; gargle tea for sore throat; cooked greens for food.

trillium, red; beths   M.
TRILLIUM ERECTUM   LILIACEAE
Tea for profuse menstruation, hemorrhages; coughs; asthma; bowel complaints; poultice for putrid ulcers, tumors, and inflamed parts; drink warm tea for change of life.

turtlehead, snake-head   M
CHELONE GLABRA   SCROPHULARIACEAE
Increases appetite; for sores or skin eruptions; fevers; worms; drink tea of blooms to move bowels gently.

twayblade   M.
LIPARIS LOESELII   ORCHIDACEAE
Root tea with ladies's tresses for urinary problems.

twin leaf   M.
JEFFERSONIA DIPHYLLA   BERBERIDACEAE
Tea for dropsy; gravel; urinary problems; externally applied to sores, ulcers and inflamed parts.

twisted stalk, white mandarin   M.
STREPTOPUS AMPLEXIFOLIUS   LILIACEAE
S. ROSEUS
Cooked greens for food.

umbrella leaf, large waterleaf   M.
DIPHYLLEIA CYMOSA   BERBERIDACEAE

Tea for small-pox; diaphoretic; diuretic; antiseptic.

venus flytrap -O.
DIONAEA MUSCIPULA DIONAEACEAE
Chew small piece and spit on bait for fishing.

venus' looking-glass M.
SPECULARIA PERFOLIATA Intro. CAMPANULACEAE
Roots an ingredient in drink for dyspepsia from overeating.

vervane M.
VERBENA HASTATA VERBENACEAE
Use leaves, seeds and roots for emetic; one quart proof spirits, one handful roots, for
dropsy; flux, old bowel complaints; early stages of fever; sudorific; good for colds;
coughs; female obstructions and afterpains; root is astringent; tonic; tonic for breast
complaints; to strengthen stomach; with other ingredients for flux; dysentery.

vetch, carolina M.
VICIA CAROLINIANA FABACEAE
Decoction for dyspepsia; back pains; rubbed on stomach cramps; rubbed on ball
palyers to render their muscles tough; for blacks; with sweet everlasting for
rheumatism; ingredient in medicine for local pains, muscular cramps and twitching;
ingredient with virginia pine and sweet apple in drink for ball players' wind during
game.

vetch, crown; black little M.
CORONILLA VARIA Intro. FABACEAE
Emetic; crush and rub on rheumatism or cramps.

violet — birdfoot, common blue, downy yellow, marsh blue, pansy, yellow, johnny-
jump-up — false blue
VIOLA PEDATA VIOLACEAE
V. PAPILIONACEA
V. PUBESCENS
V. CUCULLATA
V. ROTUNDIFOLIA
V. RAFINESQUIL
Bind leaves on head for headache; poultice of crushed root for boils; spray tea up
nose for catarrh; soak corn in root tea before planting to keep off insects; tea with
sugar for cough; tea for colds; tea for dysentery; tea for blood; tea for spring tonic.

viper's bugloss, blue devil, blue weed, their he ac M,O.
ECHIUM VULGARE Intro. BORAGINACEAE
Ingredient in drink for milky urine; seeds were formerly ma ie i. 'o beads.

virginia creeper M.
PARTHENCISSUS QUINQUEFOLIA VITACEAE
Tea for yellow jaundice.

virgin's bower, clematis, little vine M.
CLEMATIS VIRGINIANA RANUNCULACEAE
Root tea for kidneys; ingredient in green corn medicine; warm infusion with milk
weed for bachache; root infusion for stomach trouble; tea for nerves.

walink, highland fern M.
POLYPODIUM VIRGINIANUM POLYPODIACEAE

Poultice for inflamed swellings and wounds; tea for hives.

walking-fern, walking leaf   M.
ASPLENIUM RHIZOPHYLLUM   ASPLENIACEAE
Ingredient in cure for swollen breasts.

walnut, black   M,F,D,O.
JUGLANS NIGRA   JUGLANDACEAE
Bark used cautiously in medicine because it is poisonous. Inner bark infusion for smallpox; tea of leaves for goiter; chew bark for toothache; tea to wash sores; nuts for food; bark, roots, husks for brown dye; leaves for greenish dye; carving; gunstocks; furniture.

walnut, white; butternut   M,F,D,O.
JUGLANS CINEREA   JUGLANDACEAE
Pills from inner bark as cathartic; bark infusion of this wild cherry, persimmon and alder for toothache; bark tea to check bowels; nuts for food; young root yields black dye; bark dye is brown; lumber.

wa-ne-gi-dun, angelica, lovage, nondo   -F.
LIGUSTICUM CANADENSE   APIACEAⱵ
Cooked greens for food.

watercress   -F.
NASTURTIUM OFFICINALE   Intro.   BRASSICACEAE
Greens for salad. May be eaten raw.

watermelon   M,F.
CITRULLUS VULGARIS   Intro.   CUCURBITACEAE
Seed tea for kidney trouble; chew seeds for bedwetting; food.

water plantain   M.
ALISMA SUBCORDATUM   ALISMATACEAE
Root for bowel complaints; external application to old sores, wounds, bruises, and swellings; reduces inflammation and prevents mortification of ulcers.

wild mercury   M.
ACALYPHA VIRGINICA   EUPHORBIACEAE
Root for dropsy; gravel; pox.

willow — black, mountain, weeping, white   M,O.
SALIX NIGRA   SALICACEAE
S. HUMILIS
S. BABYLONICA   Intro.
S. ALBA   Intro.
Bark for tonic; poultices; bark tea to check bowels; drink tea of inner bark for lost voice; chew root for hoarsness; ball players chew root for wind; tea for fever; bark and twigs used in basketry; boil or soak bark in water use to wash hair and make it grow.

wintergreen, mountain birch, teaberry   M,F.
GAULTHERIA PROCUMBENS   ERICACEAE
Root tea with trailing arbutus for chronic indigestion; dried leaves substitute for chewing tobacco; chew leaves for dysentery; tea for colds; chew for tender gums; food.

wintergreen, spotted; wild rats bane   M,O.
CHIMAPHILA MACULATA   ERICACEAE
Tops and roots for urinary problems; rheumatism; scrofula, cancer, ulcer externally
wash affected parts; stew in hogs lard to cure tetter and ringworm; root poultice for
pain; tea of leaves for colds and fevers; tea for milksick; tea to make baby vomit; use
to kill rats.

witch hazel   M.
HAMAMELIS VIRGINIANA   HAMAMELIDACEAE
Tea for colds; bark of this, spice wood and virginia pine needles makes tea for fevers;
tea for sore throat; tea to bathe sores and skinned places; tea for periodic pains;
bruise leaves and rub on scratches; bark tea for tuberculosis.

witherod, black haw, maple-leaved viburnum, nannyberry   M.
VIRBURNUM CASSINOIDES   CAPRIFOLIACEAE
V. PRUNIFOLIUM
V. ACERIFOLIUM
Ingredient in smallpox tea; wash sore tongue with bark infusion; bark of root is tonic
and diaphoretic; ague and fever; tea to prevent recurrent spasms.

wormwood   M.
ARTEMISIA BIENNIS   Intro.   ASTERACEAE
Poultice stomach for worms; cramps; colic; painful menstruation; sores; wounds;
put seed in molasses for worms.

yarrow   M.
ACHILLEA MILLEFOLIUM   Intro.   ASTERACEAE
Leaves are astringent; hemorrhages; spitting blood; bloody piles; bloody urine;
bowel complaints; flooding; smoke dried leaves for catarrh; drink tea for fever and
restful sleep.

yaupon, southern; cassine, dahoon   M,O.
ILEX VOMITORIA   AQUIFOLIACEAE
I. CASSINE
Used for dropsy and gravel; "black drink" tea causes sweating which purifies
physically and morally; used to evoke ecstasies; "No one is allowed to drink it in
council unless he has proved himself a brave warrior." (James Adair)

yellow-eyed grass   M.
XYRIS CAROLINIANA   XYRIDACEAE
Root steep drunk for diarrhea; good for children.

yellowroot, shrub yellow roots   M,D
XANTHORHIZA SIMPLICISSIMA   RANUNCULACEAE
Astringent and tonic; tea of root for piles; ashes burnt from greenswitch for cancer;
poultice for sore eyes; root tea for cramps; decoction with wild ginger, rattlesnake
plantain, alder and wild cherry is good blood tonic; tea for nerves; chew stem for sore
mouth and throat; crush entire plant for yellow dye.

yellow wood   -O.
CLADRASTIS LUTEA   FABACEAE
Lumber, carving.

The following plant materials used by Cherokee people could not be identified and
placed in specific categories. Perhaps you know what one or more of them are. We
would be so happy to hear from anyone able to further our identification of the

following:

ah-squah-na-ta-quah
Grows at head of small mountain streams, three to five feet high; blade similar to corn, many small dark brown roots.
Bruise root, place in cold water, use daily; diuretic, for dropsy, overfatness. — Foreman

bead wood
Drink bark tea for delayed period. — Chiltoskey

black dittany
Leaf and branch decoction; diaphoretic; for child-bed fever; colds and coughs; sweating medicine; increase urine gently and menstrual discharges. — Foreman.

buck-tree (beach)
Antiseptic; poultice for inflamed wounds, ulcers. — Foreman

Culsay-tse-e-you-stee
Grows in rich bottoms and along borders of meadows; fibrous perennial root is whitish; stem four-six inches, leaves grow out on side of stem; decoction of entire plant is infallible cure for whopping cough. — Foreman

da-yi-u-wa-yi
Fern — root ingredient in rheumatism cure — Mooney

sumach, black
For clap; asthma or phthisic; ague and fever; gleet or ulcerated bladder; wash for foul ulcers. — Foreman

wild plantain
Used for snake bite; chew root, swallow most and apply rest to the wound, repeat as necessary. — Adair

yellow-rooted grass
Decoction for toothache — Mooney

E-gun-li
Two ferns, roots used for rheumatism. — Mooney

Indian cup-plant
Root for perspiration; for inward bruises, for fevers. — Mooney.

Indian fever root
Strong root decoction emetic; purgative; for colds; female obstructions. — Mooney

Oo-na-ker-oo-nah-sta-tse
Small white tender looking root, never larger than pea; roots have tiny balls that looks like artichokes; 6-12 inch stems divides into 2 or 3 stems each with 3 light green oval, smooth leaves; similar to cholera morbus with different roots. Tonic for weak people.

BIBLIOGRAPHY

Adair, J. 1775. HISTORY OF THE AMERICAN INDIANS. LONDON: E. and C. Dilly

Banks, Wm. H. Jr. 1953. ETHNOBOTANY OF THE CHEROKEE INDIANS. UNIV. TENN.

BARTON, B. S. 1789. Collections for an essay toward a materia medica of the United States. 1. Philadelphia: Way and Groff.

Bartram, W. 1791. TRAVELS OF WILLIAM BARTRAM. N. Y.: Dover reprints 1928.

Bonnefoy, A.1741-42. Journal of Antoine Bonnefoy. in Mereness, N. D., ed. TRAVELS IN THE AMERICAN COLONIES. N. Y.: Mac Millan. 1916.

Chamberlain, L. S. 1901. Plants used by the Indians of Eastern North America. American Naturalist, 35(409):1-10

Chiltoskey, M. U. 1972. CHEROKEE WORDS WITH PICTURES. Asheville, N. C.: Stephens Press.

Cobb, B. 1963, FIELD GUIDE TO THE FERNS. Boston: Houghton-Mifflin Co.

Collier, P. 1973. WHEN SHALL THEY REST? N. Y.: Dell.

Core, E. L. 1967. Ethnobotany of the Southern Appalachian aborigines. Economic Botany, 21: 199-214.

Fernald, M. L. 1958. GRAY'S MANUAL OF BOTANY, 8th ed. N. Y.: American Book Co.

Gambold, A. 1818. Plants of the Cherokee Country in Witthoft, J. 1947. An early Cherokee ethnobotanical note. Journal Washington Academy Science, 37: 73-75.

Gleason, H. and A. Cronquist. 1963. MANUAL OF VASCULAR PLANTS OF NORTHEASTERN UNITED STATES AND ADJACENT CANADA. Princeton, N. J.: Von Nostrand.

Gray, A. 1887. THE ELEMENTS OF BOTANY. rev. ed. N. Y.: American Book Co.

Hale, M. E. 1969. HOW TO KNOW LICHENS. Dubuque, Ia.: W. C. Brown.

Hamel, Paul 1974. PLANTS OF THE CHEROKEES: Dept. of Rec. & Park Admin., Clemson U., Clemson, S.C.

Hesler, L. R. 1960. MUSHROOMS OF THE GREAT SMOKIES. Knoxville: Univ. Tenn. Pr.

Mooney, J. 1889. Cherokee Plant Lore. Amer. Anthropol., 2(3): 223-224

Mooney, J. 1889. MYTHS OF THE CHEROKEE and SACRED FORMULAS OF THE CHEROKEE. Nashville, Tn: Charles Elder 1972 reprint.

Mooney, J. and F. M. Olbrechts. 1932. The Swimmer manuscript: Cherokee sacred formulas and medicinal prescriptions. U. S. Bureau of American Ethnology, Bulletin 99.

Plowden, C. C. 1970. MANUAL OF PLANT NAMES. N. Y.: Philosophical Library.

Radford, A. E., H. E. Ahles, and C. R. Bell. 1968. MANUAL OF THE VASCULAR FLORA OF THE CAROLINAS. Chapel Hill: Univ. N. C. Pr.

Sharp, J. E. 1970. THE CHEROKEES PAST AND PRESENT. Cherokee, N. C.: Cherokee Pr.

Shuttleworth, F. S. and H. S. Zim. 1967. NON-FLOWERING PLANTS. N. Y.: Golden Pr.

Stupka, A. 1964. TREES, SHRUBS, AND WOODY VINES OF GREAT SMOKY MOUNTAINS NATIONAL PARK. Knoxville: Univ. Tenn. Pr.

Tankersley, L. C., Jr. 1975. Ridge Runner. Cherokee One Feather, 8(12):3. 19 MARCH 75. Reprinted from Pickens, S. C. Sentinel.

Timberlake, H. 1765. MEMOIRS OF HENRY TIMBERLAKE. N. Y.: Arno Pr. 1971.

Vega, Garcilaso de la. 1723. LA FLORIDA DEL INCA. English translation by J. G. and J. J. Varner, 1951. Austin: Univ. Texas Pr.

Ware, G. W. and J. P. McCollum. 1968. PRODUCING VEGETABLE CROPS. Danville, Il.: Interstate Printers & Publishers.

Witthoft, J. unpublished notes on Cherokee History.

Making a canoe in the old way at the Oconaluftee Indian Village. The log is a tulip poplar (LIRIODENDRON TULIPIFERA).

INDEX

66

68